Psychology After Discourse Analysis

Ian Parker has been a leading light in the fields of critical and discursive psychology for over 25 years. The *Psychology After Critique* series brings together for the first time his most important papers. Each volume in the series has been prepared by Ian Parker, features a newly written introduction and presents a focused overview of a key topic area.

Psychology After Discourse Analysis is the third volume in the series and addresses three central questions:

- How did discourse analysis develop inside psychology?
- How does discursive psychology address concerns about the traditional 'laboratory experiment' paradigm in psychology?
- What is the future for discourse analysis?

The book provides a clear account of the various forms of discourse analysis that have been used within psychology, and provides a review of their significance for a new generation of psychologists. The early chapters present a framework for understanding the origins of these various forms, as well as the differences between them. Emphasizing the gap between discursive psychology and mainstream psychology, Parker then explores relations between discourse analysis, psychoanalysis, social constructionism and the postmodern turn in the social sciences. The final chapters describe the limitations of discourse analysis and explore its flaws as a framework and as a practice, questioning its future within academia and in political and social contexts beyond psychology.

Psychology After Discourse Analysis is essential reading for students and researchers in psychology, sociology, social anthropology and cultural studies, and for discourse analysts of different traditions. It will also introduce key ideas and debates in critical psychology for undergraduates and postgraduate students across the social sciences.

Ian Parker is Professor of Management in the School of Management, University of Leicester, UK, Honorary Professor of Education in the Manchester Institute of Education, University of Manchester, UK, and Co-Director of the Discourse Unit, UK (www.discourseunit.com).

Psychology After Critique

Ian Parker has been at the centre of developments in critical and discursive psychology for over 25 years. The *Psychology After Critique* series brings together for the first time his most important and influential papers. Each volume in the series has been prepared by Ian Parker, presents a concise and focused overview of a key topic area, and includes a newly written introduction which traces the continuing impact of the 'crisis', 'deconstruction', 'discourse analysis', 'psychoanalysis' and 'Lacanian research' inside the discipline of psychology.

Volumes in the series:

Psychology After the Crisis
Scientific paradigms and political debate

Psychology After Deconstruction
Erasure and social reconstruction

Psychology After Discourse Analysis
Concepts, methods, critique

Psychology After Psychoanalysis
Psychosocial studies and beyond

Psychology After the Unconscious
From Freud to Lacan

Psychology After Lacan
Connecting the clinic and research

Psychology After Discourse Analysis
Concepts, methods, critique

Ian Parker

LONDON AND NEW YORK

First published 2015
by Routledge
27 Church Road, Hove, East Sussex BN3 2FA

and by Routledge
711 Third Avenue, New York, NY 10017

Routledge is an imprint of the Taylor & Francis Group, an informa business

© 2015 Ian Parker

The right of Ian Parker to be identified as the author of this work has been asserted by him in accordance with sections 77 and 78 of the Copyright, Designs and Patents Act 1988.

All rights reserved. No part of this book may be reprinted or reproduced or utilised in any form or by any electronic, mechanical, or other means, now known or hereafter invented, including photocopying and recording, or in any information storage or retrieval system, without permission in writing from the publishers.

Trademark notice: Product or corporate names may be trademarks or registered trademarks, and are used only for identification and explanation without intent to infringe.

British Library Cataloguing in Publication Data
A catalogue record for this book is available from the British Library

Library of Congress Cataloging in Publication Data
Parker, Ian, 1956–
  Psychology after discourse analysis : concepts, methods, critique / Ian Parker.—1st Edition.
    pages cm—(Psychology after critique)
  includes bibliographical references and index.
  1. Social psychology. 2. Discourse analysis—Psychological aspects. I. Title.
  HM1019.P375 2014
  302—dc23
  2014005507

ISBN: 978-1-84872-210-1 (hbk)
ISBN: 978-1-84872-211-8 (pbk)
ISBN: 978-1-31577-407-7 (ebk)

Typeset in Times New Roman
by Swales & Willis Ltd, Exeter, Devon

Contents

Series foreword	vi
Series preface	ix
Acknowledgements	xi
Introduction: psychology after discourse analysis	1
1 Discourse analysis: dimensions of critique in psychology	8
2 Four story-theories about and against postmodernism in psychology	28
3 Discourse analysis and psycho-analysis	44
4 Discursive complexes in material culture	63
5 Against discursive imperialism, empiricism and constructionism WITH ERICA BURMAN	76
6 Discourse analysis and micronations of the self in times of war	91
References	106
Index	119

Series foreword

In the essays collected in these six volumes Ian Parker has brought together for the first time the two radical movements that began in social psychology in the 1960s and 1970s. One of these movements was based on a critical appraisal of the defective methodology of the research programmes that emanated from mainstream American social psychologists. This was rejected for a variety of reasons by a wide variety of critics who shared the belief that people actually deal with what they take to be the meanings of what is happening around them and the significance of the arenas in which actions were performed, according to the rules and conventions of their local social order. The results of a shallow, positivistic approach to discerning the wellsprings of human social behaviour were rejected as sources of reliable knowledge. How people thought, acted, felt and perceived their worlds had little to do with how people actually lived their lives together. People in the stripped-down meaningless worlds of the social psychological experiment were not reacting to stimuli, just trying to make sense of anomic situations with whatever resources their education and history had provided them. People are not empty sites for causal processes but active agents engaged in the tasks and projects that their lives throw up.

At the same time, and for the most part independently, a different kind of criticism was emerging – a display of the moral aspects of the very kind of psychology that was rejected as unscientific by the methodological sceptics. If people believed that psychologists were unearthing the truth about how people thought and acted, then insofar as actual people were unlike this paradigm they would or should strive to achieve it. The realization that such psychology-driven workbooks of human vagaries such as the DSM series of manuals, by presenting a range of ways for human beings to live and act as disorders, defined a kind of person to be emulated who was very much like the bland artefact generated by the statistical methods of the American mainstream, all dissent and difference being ironed out in the deference to some arbitrary level of statistical significance. Critical psychology began to reveal the ways in which the power structures of society and the relations between people from different social classes were brought about. Critical psychology drew from social constructionism the principle that when you can see how something is manufactured you can change it.

The strangest of all the eccentricities of the 'main stream' was the neglect of language. It could hardly be more obvious that the main medium of social interactions is linguistic. Once that is acknowledged the way is open for another dimension – the study of the differences between the linguistically differentiated cultures of the various tribes of humankind. This was not 'cross-cultural psychology' which was merely the transfer of Western middle-class conceptions of life to shape research into the lives of people of very different ways of thinking and acting.

In this elegant introduction to the field of critical psychology Ian Parker shows how gradually but inexorably the two streams began to merge, a process that is continuing. The most striking way in which a critical psychology is currently evolving is in the development of psychology as a moral science. Tied to this insight are explicit studies of the way rights and duties come between natural and acquired tendencies to act and the possibilities that different local moral orders allow: the rapidly growing field of positioning theory.

But all was not plain sailing. The turn to deconstruction, via a reshaping of the linguistic turn to encompass the richer domain of discourse, led to the neglect of the key claim that the 'new psychology' gave socially relative and epoch-specific reliable knowledge, at least pro tem. To reclaim psychiatry from the neurochemists, the place of the active person within a local framework was an essential core to be defended. If persons fade away into clusters of locally contingent selves the key point of the reality of human agency was in danger of being lost.

The second deep insight – perhaps more important than the defence of persons, was relocation of 'mind' to the social network of meaningful interactions, the mind in society. When we learn to abstract ourselves one by one from the social nexus from which each of us emerges we bear with us the indelible mark of our cultural origins. The recoverable content of psycho-dynamics relocates the unconscious to 'what lies between'. In the end we turn back to language and relate symbolic systems not as abstract calculi obeying inbuilt species-specific rules but as the common instruments with which we manage our lives. Psychology can be nothing but the study of cultural-historical-instrumental practices of our ever-changing tribal societies.

The *Psychology After Critique* series is the comprehensive resource we have been waiting for to enable new generations not only of budding psychologists but all those who concern themselves with how we might live, to find their way through the mistakes of the positivistic illusion of a science to a just appreciation of what it might be to come to understand the myriad ways a human being can be a person among persons.

Rom Harré
Linacre College, University of Oxford, UK
Psychology Department, Georgetown University, USA

Series preface

What is psychology? Once upon a time psychologists imagined that they knew the answer to this question. Their object of study, they argued, should be the way that individuals perceive the world, think about it and act in it together with other people. Perception and thinking, in developmental and cognitive psychology, for example, was studied as if it only happened inside the heads of the experimental 'subjects' in scientific laboratories and then 'social psychology' often amounted to little more than an accumulation of the behaviour of those same atomized individuals. The idea that people talked to each other, and that this talk might actually have an effect on the way that people behaved and understood themselves was outside the frame of that kind of academic work.

This series of books is about the consequences of talk being taken seriously, the consequences for scientific investigation and for the way that many researchers today are building innovative new research projects. The discipline of psychology has been transformed since a 'paradigm crisis' erupted nearly half a century ago when pioneers in research into the role of language in thinking and behaviour picked up the thread of early 'radical psychology' critiques which homed in on the limitations of their discipline. The 'paradigm crisis' threw into question the silent world presupposed by the psychologists and launched us all into a world of intense debate over the role of language, of discourse and then of what is shut out of discourse, of the unconscious and of psychoanalysis.

These books were produced in the context of fierce arguments about methods in psychology and over the kinds of concepts we needed to develop in order to do better more radical research. The Discourse Unit was founded in Manchester as a Centre for Qualitative and Theoretical Research on the Reproduction and Transformation of Language, Subjectivity and Practice in 1990. Today it operates as an international trans-institutional collaborative centre which supports a variety of qualitative and theoretical research projects contributing to the development of radical theory and practice. The term 'discourse' is used primarily in critical hermeneutic and structuralist senses to include inquiries influenced by feminism and psychoanalysis. The centre functions as a resource base for qualitative and feminist work, as a support unit for the (re)production of radical academic theory, and as a networking centre for the development of critical perspectives in action research.

We took as our starting point the 'crisis' and the need for critical reflection on the discipline of psychology, the place of psychology and appeals to psychology in other academic disciplines. We then saw the need for a 'critical psychology' that was concerned not only with what went on inside the academic world but also with the way that psychological ideas functioned in the real world outside the universities. The books in this series are written mostly by one individual participant in those debates, but they bring together a number of different arguments for perspectives on the nature of scientific paradigms, deconstruction from literary theory, discourse analysis, psychosocial studies, psychoanalysis and clinical work that were elaborated by researchers in the Discourse Unit.

The books together trace a narrative from the early recognition that language is crucial to understand what is happening in traditional laboratory-experimental psychology – why that kind of psychology is quite useless in telling us about human action – to the development of discourse analysis and the connections with some more radical attempts to 'deconstruct' language from other neighbouring disciplines. A concern with different kinds of psychoanalytic theory – the innovative work now taking place in psychosocial studies – is then introduced to conceptualize the nature of subjectivity. But from the beginning there are some 'red threads' that lead us from the study of language and subjectivity to the study of power and ideology.

These books about psychology as an academic discipline and the increasing role of psychology in our everyday lives are also about the politics of research. And so, when we began to discuss the role of 'deconstruction' or 'psychoanalysis' in the Discourse Unit we always asked whether those other conceptual frameworks would help or hinder us in understanding the connections between knowledge and social change. The books do not pretend to be neutral disinterested description of trends of research in psychology. Our 'crisis' was always about the possibility that the turn to language would also be a turn to more politically engaged – Marxist and feminist – radical reflection on what the theories and methods conceal and what we could open up. The books are accounts of the emergence of key debates after 'the crisis' and sites of 'critical psychological' reflection on the nature of psychology itself.

Ian Parker
Professor of Management in the School of Management,
University of Leicester, and Co-Director of the Discourse Unit
(www.discourseunit.com)

Acknowledgements

This book brings together versions of papers that were either been published in scattered places and are often inaccessible or that are unpublished:

Chapter 1 was published in reduced form in 2012 as 'Discourse analysis: Dimensions of critique in psychology', in *Qualitative Research in Psychology*, 10(3), 223–239, reproduced by permission of Taylor and Francis Group, LLC, a division of informa plc; Chapter 2 was published in 2000 as 'Four story-theories about and against postmodernism in psychology', in L. Holzman and J. Morss (eds) *Postmodern Psychologies: Societal Practice and Political Life* (pp. 29–48) by Routledge, reproduced by permission of Taylor and Francis Group, LLC, a division of informa plc; Chapter 3 was published in 1997 as 'Discourse analysis and psycho-analysis', in the *British Journal of Social Psychology*, 36, 479–495, reproduced by permission of John Wiley and Sons; Chapter 4 was published in 1995 as 'Discursive complexes in material culture', in J. Haworth (ed.) *Psychological Research: Innovative Methods and Strategies* (pp. 185–196) by Routledge, reproduced by permission of Taylor and Francis Group, LLC, a division of informa plc; Chapter 5, which was co-authored with Erica Burman, was published in 1993 as 'Against discursive imperialism, empiricism and constructionism: Thirty-two problems with discourse analysis', in E. Burman and I. Parker (eds) *Discourse Analytic Research: Repertoires and Readings of Texts in Action* (pp. 155–172) published by Routledge, reproduced by permission of Taylor and Francis Group, LLC, a division of informa plc. I have modified some formulations in the published papers and excluded extraneous material. I am, as ever, grateful to Erica Burman and my colleagues in the international network around the Discourse Unit for their critical comments and support during the preparation of this volume. The mistakes must surely in some way be theirs too.

> Every effort has been made to contact the copyright holders for all third-party materials used in this book. Please advise the publisher of any errors or omissions if you are a copyright holder.

Introduction
Psychology after discourse analysis

This book, the third in the series *Psychology After Critique*, explores the impact of discourse analysis as one of the most radical methodological developments in the discipline in the wake of the 'paradigm crisis' in psychology. Competing conceptions of research in psychology have emerged in recent years, and the strengthening of qualitative research before, and then with increasing influence alongside, and now after the emergence of discourse analysis as a specific approach, enables us to shift from a link between method and discipline to a new, more fruitful connection between method and innovation (Banister *et al.*, 2011).

When we founded the Discourse Unit in 1990 we took the study of 'discourse' as our focus because it seemed to us then that the most radical stance we could adopt towards the discipline would be to turn around and examine the accounts that psychologists gave of other people's behaviour as sets of 'discourses' rather than as scientific facts. In the 'new paradigm' researchers had argued for a turn to language which valued the stories ordinary people – the 'non-psychologists' as they are commonly thought of – told about themselves (Harré and Secord, 1972). These researchers drew on structuralist ideas about language, but paid keen attention to the question of human agency. They thus combined an attention to the way little social worlds (like classrooms and football terraces) were structured with a humanist sympathy for the way people in those social worlds made meaning. In this way, the 'new paradigm' continued in the line of the 'modern' Western Enlightenment project of mainstream psychology.

Discourse analysis took this work forward in a 'turn to discourse' that focused attention on the many competing structures of language and the way these enabled speakers to engage in the 'social construction' of reality. This was an approach that was more in tune with so-called 'post-structuralist' ideas, and was even seen by some supporters and critics as being 'postmodern' (Parker, 2002). The development of discourse analysis also facilitated the uptake of radical theoretical accounts of subjectivity, including from new forms of psychoanalysis. This book should be read alongside other books in the series that deal specifically with the crisis debates, deconstruction and aspects of psychoanalytic and 'psychosocial' research. This introduction, and then the chapters in the book are concerned with how discourse analysis developed inside psychology, what discursive psychology had to say about critical debates in the discipline, and where discourse analysis is going now.

The 'turn to discourse'

The point has been made by historians that the discipline of psychology is held together not so much by shared conceptions of its object of study – the psychology textbooks are testimony to lack of agreement about what we should be describing – but by its *method* (Rose, 1985). Agreement about the way we should study the many different things that are taken to be part of 'psychology' defines it as a separate domain of research, and also not-coincidentally characterizes it as a discipline, as a form of discipline. A 'method' is taken to include a certain kind of 'procedure' that is brought to bear on what were for many years called our 'subjects', and strict adherence to this procedure was thought to guarantee that the study could be replicated by other researchers. In this way the motif of 'prediction and control' applied not only to the behaviour of subjects but to the researchers as subjects themselves (Parker, 2007a).

In the positivist laboratory-experimental paradigm, a paradigm that to all intents and purposes was treated as necessarily 'quantitative' because it was assumed that only that which was measurable was worth noticing, different methodological frameworks (ranging from recording reaction times to gathering responses to questionnaires) were expressed as method in specific steps (Harré and Secord, 1972). The steps should, as part of a method, follow a sequence in order to produce a result that would only differ according to conditions under which the steps were followed or the characteristics of the subjects altered. The criteria used to assess the value of the research then logically rested on the reliability and validity of the procedures, including those embedded in the research instruments, the apparatus used to measure behaviour (Burman and MacLure, 2005). It was only the fixed nature of the grid used and followed by researchers that could ensure that it would be recognizable to other researchers, recognizable as psychology as such.

A consequence of these notions of method, steps and criteria for research was that psychology had to factor language itself into the discipline as something recognizably psychological, as psychology compatible with the forms of discipline that studied it. Language then came to be described as another sequence of variables that must be segmented into forms of expression that could be measured by the researcher. One way of doing this is to treat language as a form of 'verbal behaviour', which was the way of the behaviourists (Skinner, 1957). With the development of cognitive models a corresponding cognitivist conception of language emerged which moderated that behaviourist account. However, this cognitive conception simply treated elements of language as behavioural sequences which contained within them the packets of communication that were expressed by the speaker (or writer) and then unwrapped by the listener (or reader) (Easthope, 1990).

Discourse analysis marks a conceptual break from behavioural and cognitive models of language as expression of response to stimuli or as communication of ideas from inside the head of an individual to others. Crucially for psychology, and as a preliminary requirement of research into discourse, it breaks from methodological assumptions in the old paradigm, to carry out its work in an entirely different, qualitative, paradigm (Harré, 2004). The extent to which the study of language now takes its place in qualitative research as a paradigm concerned with meaning rather than behaviour, with interpretation rather than measurement, and with an ethos of accountability rather than deception that marked the old paradigm is a matter of debate, an open question (Reason and Rowan, 1981). How we answer that question will depend on the specific methodological frameworks we adopt and how we put those methodological frameworks into practice as method in discourse analysis.

Critical discursive psychology

For the purposes of our exploration of the field of discourse analysis, the following principles will be important. The first principle for innovative discursive research is that in place of fixed method abstracted from context, we are concerned from the beginning of our work with the phenomena we study as *historically* constituted. This means that even before the analysis begins we are oriented to noticing how the phenomenon has come into being and how it changes.

The second principle is that, in place of simple steps that should be followed, we know that we must bring to bear upon the phenomenon a *theoretical* understanding. A theory or cluster of competing theories always guides a researcher, whether these are implicit or explicit. In much traditional research in psychology they are either borrowed from the existing reductive models of the person or unthinkingly adapted from the commonsensical images of the person that surround the discipline. Our task is to turn what is implicit into that which is explicit, and to develop theory that is useful for our purposes in research.

The third principle is to embed some kind of account of *subjectivity* into the research process, and even if that account is not immediately developed as a theory of the subjectivity of those inhabiting the discourse we describe, it should at least include the subjectivity of the researcher in forms of reflexivity. We notice and describe the world from particular positions, and the position of the researcher needs to be specified at some point in some kind of reflexive analysis so that the claims that are made are more readily assessable by the reader of the research.

Once history, theory and subjectivity are brought centre-stage in research, we are able to appreciate how innovation becomes more important to good research than discipline. Each piece of new research that locates what it studies in history, that brings theory to bear on the way it is conceptualized and that includes the subjectivity of the researcher must *invent* its methodology anew. Good research takes previous studies into account but refuses to simply replicate the method in a sequence of steps that obey a fixed grid of criteria that conform to the way that the discipline of psychology defines its objects. Existing approaches to discourse analysis are, as we shall see, internally contradictory, and are all the better for that, and it is from that existing work and the contradictions that define them that a researcher will be able to develop new studies and new methodologies (Banister *et al.*, 2011). In the course of the book I mark the boundaries between forms of discourse analysis in the hope that researchers taking up some of these ideas in their own research will disturb those boundaries and invent new connections between the concepts.

Discourse analysis now: self-critique and trans-disciplinary research practice

Discourse analysis was already from its origins in such interdisciplinary projects as the 'Sociology of Scientific Knowledge', intensely reflexive (Potter and Wetherell, 1987; Woolgar, 1988). Discourse analysts were open to thinking about 'science' as a social construction, about their own disciplines (such as psychology) as social constructions, and even about their own practice as socially constructed. It was that self-critical aspect of the approach that led some psychologists to assume that the approach was 'relativist' or even 'postmodern'. I must admit that I did think at one point that a 'realist' approach in discursive research was a progressive alternative to relativism (Parker, 1992a).

I was wrong, and see now that thorough-going relativism in psychology of the kind promoted by the discourse analysts, including my friends and colleagues in the Discourse and Rhetoric Group (DARG) at Loughborough, was the best way of dismantling the scientific truth claims and managerial ambitions of psychology. But where do we go now after self-critique? The trajectory of this book is towards a more sustained attention to the role of psychology in the world outside the academic discipline, to 'psychologization' in culture, and to the activities of ordinary people as they themselves carry out forms of discourse analysis. This leads us to look carefully at boundaries in research, and at the way different kinds of boundary raise questions about the nature of our different domains of academic work and their relation to practice.

The first boundary is the boundary between psychology as a distinct discipline that concerns itself with the nature of individual thinking and behaviour on the one hand, and, on the other, 'psychological culture' as the field of application and elaboration of psychology, a field within which psychologists have to compete against a variety of popular commonsensical accounts of how people think and behave (Gordo and De Vos, 2010). This is the boundary between those who work as theorists and practitioners in the 'psy-complex', those who have expert understanding, and the people who puzzle about what the psychologists know about them. This boundary is discursively organized, and it is indeed discursively organized within material institutional practices.

What we psychologists think we know about the 'nature' of human psychology is culturally specific, and certain kinds of academic and professional psychology hold sway (e.g. Burman, 2008a). This, both locally in each distinct sector of the capitalist economy by virtue of the imperative to manage the work and leisure pursuits of normal folk as well as the abnormal ones who will not play the game, and globally under contemporary neoliberal forms of imperialism through the hegemony of specific definitions of what counts as human labour power, what is countable as consumer preference, and what can be accumulated by those who have sufficient capital. The key point here is that there is no 'psychology' as such, only historically constituted psychologies that have already mutated many times and will be transformed when we transform the discursive boundary between the psychologists and the so-called 'non-psychologists'.

The second boundary is the boundary between discourse analysis as a distinct academic practice that concerns itself with forms of language and the way it is structured in texts on the one hand and, on the other, 'discursive culture' as the field of argument, rhetorical contest and political debate within which the discourse analysts find themselves jostling against a variety of popular commonsensical ideas about how people talk and write and why it matters. This, then, is the boundary between the discourse analysts in academic departments and people outside who are already carrying out forms of discourse analysis as part of their critical and disruptive readings of texts. The key point here is that this boundary is also discursively organized, and this discursive organization is, once again, woven into material institutional practices.

This means that discourse analysts need to challenge how that boundary between the inside and outside of their discipline distributes certain forms of expertise so that certain kinds of practice inside the discipline is regulated and certain kinds of practice outside the discipline is rendered invisible. There is no 'discourse analysis' as such, only historically constituted forms of close reading, reinterpretation and rewriting, forms that either serve to embed our understanding of language in certain dominant cultural practices or enable us to open the way to a transformation of language. This is where we come to a point of intersection between the two boundaries.

When I refer to 'language' it should be clear by now that it is as discursive practice, and so to speak of 'critical discursive practice' is to take a stance towards it (Burman et al., 1996). Critical discursive practice is a domain of work that is important to many 'critical psychologists' because it enables us to turn around and treat our own discipline as a collection of texts susceptible to deconstruction (Parker, 2002). One activity at the intersection between psychology and discourse analysis, or at the intersection between the two boundaries that structure how each disciplinary practice maintains itself, is where we critical psychologists try to make sure that critical colleagues outside psychology do not look to us, to any of us, to supply the 'psychological' explanation, to fill in the gap that those from other disciplines think it is necessary to fill (Parker, 2005a).

But there is another activity which is just as important, which is where we attend to the way that certain psychological assumptions, culturally and historically specific assumptions, reappear in work on discourse. We need to attend to the way that discourse work specifies forms of behaviour and forms of interiority, and the way it takes certain 'psychological' notions for granted. Of course, discourse theory has been able to distance itself from the idea that language simply enables thoughts to be conveyed from one head to another, coded and decoded by sender and receiver, and so susceptible to decoding by an astute analyst (Easthope, 1990). There are still discourse analysts in psychology who do think that when they study language they are also necessarily revealing underlying thought processes in the author of a spoken or written text, and that is certainly a problem we still need to tackle on our side of the intersection between our different areas of work. However, what concern us here are the other less obvious temptations to psychologize that seep into discourse work and that would then seep back into psychology that drew upon that work. Notions of cognitive processing, schemata, interpellation, phenomenological immediacy and embodied meaning are still too easily to hand in discourse and need to be treated with care, with suspicion (Parker, 1992a).

It is not surprising that such temptations should be so available, so pressing; not so much because the psychologists themselves have been such good salesmen but because they too draw upon and feed back to us different forms of contemporary psychological culture that make individual thought processes seem to be the point of explanation for patterns of exploitation and resistance (Parker, 1989). Contemporary psychological culture, which is globalizing the domain of 'psychology' as a field of explanation in part through the spread of the English language, is a potent structuring force, a system of discursive practices interlaced with global and local political-economic processes, and it needs to be tackled as a powerful phenomenon by critical discourse analysts. Let us turn to some examples of psychological culture that discourse analysts need to tackle. Two graphic examples will illustrate some practical interventions in discourse by those outside academic discourse analysis.

First, the 'London Psychogeographical Association' has members who have been active in the main anti-capitalist protests over the past decade or so, but their own critical discursive practice is an intervention that is designed to shake up the form and content of debate. One of their initiatives is 'three-sided football', something that has profound implications for the way we think about boundaries and the opposition between different groupings, whether they are academic groupings or disciplinary groupings. One participant proclaims that 'In England, the resistance will be led by the London Psychogeographical Association, who will use games of three-sided football to free people from the shackles of dualistic thinking' (London Psychogeographical Association, 1997: 88).

A second example, which owes something to situationist interventions into public texts, is 'Glop Art'. This refers to the activity of sticking bits of chewing gum on advertising posters in the London Underground, an activity that has also provoked some agonizing among its participants about the extra work it might entail for the cleaners. Nevertheless, the strategic addition of a bit of gum intervenes in the image and changes it; so it is claimed, for example, that 'Glop Art represents the cutting edge of critical thinking among outsider artists whose opposition to all forms of capitalist culture manifests itself as a self-conscious ethical positioning' (Blissett, 1997: 199).

These practices refuse to participate in the usual ameliorative procedures of academic life, even in those procedures that pretend to be the most critical, including in 'critical psychology' (Parker, 2011a). There is no 'advice' to those in power as to how messages could be decoded or reformatted, and no dialogue about how signifiers could be rearticulated. Operating at the intersection between a refusal of academic discourse analysis and a refusal of academic psychology, they raise a question as to how we, on this side of our boundary, will use our position in solidarity with them, will use our own academic position to transform the cultural practices that we participate in.

1 Discourse analysis
Dimensions of critique in psychology

In the early years of the Discourse Unit we spent many hours discussing with students and colleagues how to make sense of the different 'introductions' to discourse analysis that were each giving competing accounts of what the approach was. In many cases these introductions were from different disciplinary contexts – linguists, literary theory, philosophy, sociology and political theory – and as time went on the appearance of a tradition of discourse analysis in psychology helped matters a bit. But not much, because there are now still many versions of discourse analysis in psychology that carry with them assumptions from the host discipline from which they were gathered.

This chapter tackles that confusion by providing a map by which researchers might at least be able to identify where the different accounts of discourse analysis are coming from. It provides a systematic account of eight different forms of discourse analysis organized into four different levels of approach, ranging from the micro-interpersonal level to historical-political level. This is a longer version of a paper that was eventually cut to size for publication in a qualitative research in psychology journal.

Discourse analysis in psychology provides a range of conceptual and methodological resources for thinking critically about the discipline of psychology. These conceptual and methodological resources also reorient researchers in the discipline away from a search for causes of behaviour inside the heads of individuals to social contexts in which human beings construct and challenge what has been presented to them as 'facts' about their nature or

> possibilities for change. Discourse analysis has sometimes even been treated as synonymous with 'critical psychology', and enabled politically progressive alternative approaches to subjectivity, so this paper also reviews connections with 'critical psychological' approaches and more broadly with dimensions of critique in research.

Research that aims to connect discourse analysis with critical psychology faces at least two problems. The first is that, as is the case for the forms of language it studies, 'discourse analysis' itself poses a choice for researchers who use it to describe or change the world, a choice which hinges on the idea that we always either reproduce or transform phenomena when we describe them. There are forms of discourse analysis that aim to merely describe forms of language, and so they 'reproduce' what they find. Against this politically conservative choice, we are concerned here with discourse analysis that transforms the world, the kind of analysis that connects interpretation with change. The phrase 'reproduction or transformation' is borrowed from a 'realist' tradition of inquiry (Bhaskar, 1986). That tradition is sometimes pitted against discourse analysis, and it does draw attention to the importance of 'structure' as a condition for or constraint upon human agency (Parker, 1988).

The second problem is that there is a host of different approaches to discourse analysis, and each approach is governed by a series of conceptual and methodological terms which themselves orient the researcher to attend to specific delimited aspects of language. This array of different approaches causes much confusion to a researcher beginning to learn to notice the structuring force of language and wanting to study it. Our response to this diversity in the field of discourse analysis is to treat this as an opportunity, and to clarify the role of different approaches in order to map the field. A critical psychologist could then make use of different elements of the approach and formulate their own research questions and possible ways of answering them.

I will focus on eight different approaches to discourse analysis, and our journey through these approaches, described in such a way as to emphasize choices about 'levels' of analysis, will take us through dimensions of research that connect in different ways with political and ideological questions. One reason there are so many varieties of discourse analysis is that there has been a focus on language in research that has taken different forms in different disciplines. This disciplinary separation can serve as an obstacle for those wanting to carry out interdisciplinary or, as we would prefer to say, 'trans-disciplinary' research (Curt, 1994). We are concerned with discourse analysis in psychology here, and so that also immediately brings us to the question of 'reproduction and transformation'. Then we are able to focus on how the discipline reproduces certain assumptions about method and how critical psychology needs to transform those assumptions (Parker, 2007a).

We will move up through four different 'levels' of analysis, beginning with the smallest-scale level that is usually treated as the domain of 'psychology', and at each level we will notice the way that a particular approach either attends to the dimension of time or space. We begin with the lowest-order conceptions of time and space that define how individuals relate to one another moment by moment and in small self-contained interaction, and trace our way up to include study of larger temporal sequences and social activity. We will oscillate between an attention to time and attention to space in this account in which we designate each approach by a two- or three-letter acronym (TLA).

Little things in context

As we begin with a focus on the kinds of discourse analysis that concentrates on little sequences of interaction in little spaces, it should be emphasized that we do not assume that bigger is better, that larger-scales of analysis are more politically progressive. There are implications here for our understanding of psychology and for the development of critical psychology in work at a micro-level as much as that at a macro-level of research. We begin with the dimension of time.

1 In time: CA

The first approach, Conversation Analysis (CA), is extremely small-scale in its temporal scope, and has found its way into psychology from across the disciplinary borders with what is sometimes known as 'micro-sociology'.

Conversation Analysis is devoted to detailed description of formal properties of talk, and builds upon the lectures of Harvey Sacks (1992). In the apparently most simple formulations that Sacks analyses – such as 'The baby cried. The mommy picked it up.' – Sacks (1972) teases apart the mutual implication of subjects ordered around social categories. Attention to 'membership categorization devices' has spawned a separate 'Membership Categorization Analysis' (MCA) strand of work that already begins to show us how micro-interaction replicates social structures (Hester and Eglin, 1997).

In CA, talk, in conversations or in other sequences that maintain or 'repair' the orderliness of everyday interaction, is unpicked and marked in a close reading of transcripts using a specific vocabulary (Sacks *et al.*, 1974); this includes 'pre-sequencing' to initiate a conversation or new topic, 'adjacency pairs' to describe how participants arrange their turns to speak, and 'preference organization' to describe how some responses which agree with or accept the action performed before it are apparently more smoothly undertaken (Atkinson and Heritage, 1984).

The orderliness and repair of what is sometimes called 'naturally occurring' conversation can be used to show how emotion that seems to disrupt talk is managed in therapy (Peräkylä *et al.*, 2008). In forms of CA treated as a version of discourse analysis in psychology there has been an extension of the approach to include detailed transcription of non-verbal interaction, such as crying (Hepburn, 2004).

CA is not behaviourist as such, but it is concerned with the form of talk rather than content, and this is something that separates it from other approaches to discourse analysis. It is precisely this behaviourally oriented aspect of the approach, to the forms of order that can be observed and described in extremely detailed transcription of behaviour that has set the battle lines between CA as such and those who have tried to extend it to account for wider structural issues, of the organization of power between men and women, for example. Hence complaints that so-called 'Feminist Conversation Analysis' (FCA) (Kitzinger, 2000) enables the leakage into the analysis of illicit content, of interpretation that is theoretically or politically informed (Wowk, 2007). FCA does allow for connections between the micro-level of interaction and societal processes, for analysis of the reproduction and transformation of the social order (Whelan, 2012). Anecdotal accounts mingled in with the analysis are thus particularly vexing for those who want to keep the analysis strictly in line with Sacks' prescriptions (Kitzinger, 2000).

Methodologically, Conversation Analysis in psychology fits very neatly with the empiricist tradition in the discipline in the English-speaking world and so this means that it is also quite conservative. An emphasis on 'transcription' as part of the method is evidence of this (Potter, 1998). However, apart from FCA (which, probably for tactical reasons, insists that it is also a rigorous empirical analysis that does not inject its own content into its readings of interaction), CA does connect with critical perspectives in 'respecifying', at least, what are usually taken to be internal 'cognitive' procedures in psychology as properties of publically accountable shared interaction (Edwards, 1997).

We can make use of this, and alongside the already existing analyses of the ordering of gender and sexuality in this tradition of work, there is the basis of something that is almost already 'critical psychology' (Gough and McFadden, 2001). However, the aversion of Conversation Analysis to theory means that it cannot take this respecification to the level of critique of psychology as such, and here it is as trapped in its own level of analysis as the actual empirical work it carries out. CA also guards its own expertise, in production and reading of transcription, and has no interest in engaging those it studies in interpretation of their own lives. There is also effectively a strict line of sub-disciplinary separation between its approach to linear ordered interaction and more phenomenologically oriented approaches in micro-sociology that are concerned with how people inhabit space with others as mutually recognized subjects, to which we turn next.

2 In space: EM

The second approach, ethnomethodology (EM), was developed by Harold Garfinkel (1967) as an approach to the question of order in the social world that already insisted, as a first principle, that the specification of this order was not the task of some putative expert who was able to divine the rules that were being followed from the outside, but was a task that was 'accomplished' by the members of the group concerned themselves. This approach actually preceded CA, and sometimes in psychology the two approaches are run together, as if CA enables a formalization of EM (Rapley, 2012). As we would expect from an approach more indebted to phenomenology, there is a concern in this approach with content rather than simply with form (Heritage, 1984); and unlike CA, Garfinkel was interested in how order could be revealed by 'insiders' refusing to conform to taken-for-granted behaviour and by such 'garfinkeling', revealing what rules were operating to hold a little social world in place (Filmer, 1972). The three elements compressed into this term 'ethnomethodology' function as a demand that 'sociologists' who want to privilege their own accounts of an overarching social order back off from everyday life-worlds.

A first element 'ethno' characterizes the particular little social world in which subjects constitute themselves in relation to others they recognize as like themselves. So even at this level of definition of a community and its boundaries there are epistemological and ontological stakes as to who will be responsible for and implement such a definition. Knowledge and being are woven together, and it is here that 'Membership Categorization Analysis' (MCA) raises a question for the discourse analyst about how understanding of this or that 'ethnographic' category should be elaborated, and MCA itself begins to attach itself more to EM than to CA (Hansen, 2005).

The 'method' element of ethnomethodology concerns the ways in which members of the particular space they inhabit bring it into being and maintain it through particular practices. All of the kinds of procedures described by CA, for example, will serve to initiate new members and render meaningful to them the order that they themselves must also take responsibility for keeping going. The jargon terms that CA uses are elaborated by outsiders, and EM is concerned, instead, with the accomplishment of sense through the practical reasoning of those inside the space they focus upon in any particular study.

The third element, which is made visible by the 'ology' part of the term, concerns the way in which everyday life needs to be theoretically elaborated by participants in order for it to be made meaningful to them. This 'ology' does not refer to what the micro-sociologist does in their application of 'ethnomethodology', but to how the micro-social order is achieved and reflected upon, and reconstituted by that very process of reflection, by those who must be accorded the status of subjects rather than objects of inquiry. It is their 'ology' that is at stake here, not that of the psychologist.

This defence of the 'ethnomethodology' of those who inhabit what they themselves take to be their own social space entails a refusal of terms of description given by outsiders, such as sociologists or psychologists, but it does force the question as to what domain the 'ology' that 'psychology' is concerned with actually applies to. This is where EM has become a conceptual resource for the Sociology of Scientific Knowledge, and the work of Bruno Latour (2012) which bore fruit in Actor Network Theory, for example, was influenced by Garfinkel. Scientific sense-making procedures in laboratory life are viewed as exactly that, the production of an 'ethnomethodology' by those concerned in the community of scientists, and, by the same token, the 'psychologists' accomplishments pertain to their own life-worlds rather than those operating in what they imagine to be the 'real world' outside (Woolgar, 1988).

There is a connection here again with specific attempts by feminist researchers to open this analysis to broader social processes; for example, to make intelligible the procedures by which someone might be marked out as 'mentally ill', making this intelligible without endorsing those procedures (Smith, 1978). Here there is a concern with something very like the giving of 'voice' to those who use mental health services, valuing their own terms of description rather than imposing another set of categories. This chimes with the feminist 'standpoint' perspective, the argument that those who suffer power see its operations more clearly (Harding, 2003). At the same time, this phenomenological defence of the life-world of those subject to academic redescription, which we could see as a first step to valuing the forms of discourse analysis that are carried out by people themselves as part of their everyday activities of making sense, also raises the same problems as those in the mental health system survivor literature. A 'voice' may not be enough without a theoretical grasp of the nature of the oppression it may really be speaking of (Cresswell and Spandler, 2009).

EM typically avoids this next step, from voice to theory because of its methodological emphasis on 'description', just as CA tries to avoid the use of theory in its own translation of experience into the particular format employed in transcripts of naturally occurring conversation. In this way, the micro-level of sequences of interaction or the shape of a life-world is maintained, sealed off from anything larger than can be empirically captured or phenomenologically grasped by subjects as an accomplishment. Discourse analysts who want to move up a scale to comprehend the structuring of the grounds of experience need to turn to ideas from other approaches.

Grounds of experience

The classic example puzzled over by Sacks (1972) – 'The baby cried. The mommy picked it up.' – is not actually embedded in a 'conversation' at all, but it does already have the structure of narrative, posing a question about what is happening, what should be done, and what kinds of subjects participate in such activities. As such, the statement is a story that also performs normative patterns and dominant themes in contemporary child-rearing practices (Burman, 2008a). When 'discourse analysis' was first introduced to British social psychology, the notion that there is something beyond immediate interaction in discourse was configured in terms of 'interpretative repertoires' (Potter and Wetherell, 1987). Two complementary approaches to discourse, one tracking the narrative dimension as a temporal structure and the other exploring the space of possible available meanings in which such stories could be told, are Narrative Analysis and Thematic Analysis.

3 In time: NA

In its simplest form, Narrative Analysis (NA) aims to produce a form of account of individual life experience in which there is a linear sequence so that the reader can recognize the structuring of life events as being rather like that of a book. This sequence may even be anticipated in the research process itself so that the interviewee is invited to structure their story with a beginning, a middle and an end (Crossley, 2000).

The way this sequence is conceptualized, for the participants in the research as much as for the researchers themselves, will affect the kinds of accounts that appear. For example, if the research is aiming to produce a life-story, then the account is likely to draw upon and then map itself into normative developmental patterns, perhaps with the interviewee being given space to talk about how his or her own life departs from those patterns. If the research is focusing on the effects of particular life-changing events, then the time before the event, the event itself and the period after it may correspond to current psychological theories of 'trauma' or allow for alternative narratives that revolve around the event to be produced. What the researcher wants the interviewee to speak about will always lead to other issues that may be more important in their life being sidelined (Billig, 1987).

In either case, the structure of a narrative provides a frame for different kinds of content to be organized by the speaker, and by the researcher, so that the account is rendered intelligible. The key issue for a critical psychologist in either case, of course, is whether 'narrative' simply operates as a frame, which can then itself be thrown into question, or whether it tempts the researcher to import their own psychological theories that too neatly fit in with the narrative format and then confirm dominant normative theories.

For example, NA has been one of the arenas in which versions of psychoanalysis have been employed. Then 'Free Associative Narrative Inquiry' (FANI), unlike Melanie Klein's version of psychoanalysis which provides the 'root metaphors' for this approach to discourse (and for which it is the patient that free associates on the couch), involves free association by the researcher about the stories told to them (Hollway and Jefferson, 2000). Like CA, there is then reluctance to feed back the interpretations that are made, and the understandable claim is that such interpretations might be disturbing to the interviewees. The danger is that the normative aspect of narrative is emphasized, and then also a corresponding psychological theory that thinks that it has something to say about the underlying nature of what is termed the 'defended subject'.

In more critical vein, psychology itself can be conceptualized as a set of narratives into which the researcher embeds their own career, structuring their activity by way of a search for clues to unsolved puzzles in line with a detective narrative, or reflecting on personal experience as the ground from which to explore an issue in line with an autobiographical narrative, or engaging in more speculative and fantastic alternatives that break from present-day models in line with a kind of science fiction narrative (Squire, 1990). Narratives are here seen as elements of cultural production that individuals may draw upon to make sense of their lives (Squire, 2000). This way of approaching narrative treats it as but one kind of time against which alternative kinds of time might be envisaged (Frosh, 2002). This links with innovations in clinical practice that emerged from the domain of social work that sometimes go under the name of 'narrative therapy' (Parker, 1999c).

Narrative therapy is a kind of Narrative Analysis in which the subjects become active participants in the process of discourse analysis, encouraged to reflect upon their problems in narrative terms and so to ask what discourses of pathology have recruited them into particular kinds of stories about the lives (Monk *et al.*, 1997). There is then a shift from descriptive–prescriptive research into a methodological concern with 'interpretation' and then to something that would more closely correspond to what is sometimes called 'action research' in which participants define and redefine the nature of the problem and what can be done to tackle it (Kagan and Burton, 2000).

4 In space: TA

In the case of Thematic Analysis (TA), the linear narrative dimension may appear as one of a number of different 'themes', but these themes are seen as operating across discursive space that does not necessarily correspond to the life-worlds of particular individuals. Thematic Analysis itself could be seen, even more explicitly than in other forms of discourse analysis, as a space of debate in which there are a number of methodological choices rather than a single prescriptive method (Braun and Clarke, 2006). When the researcher makes these choices they then connect with other research traditions that operate alongside and in tension with discourse analysis. With each connection, the TA researcher is also led away from fundamental premises of discourse analysis.

TA often functions in psychology as a fall-back option, and as a retreat to commonsensical approaches to meaning when Discourse Analysis was viewed as more difficult because it broke from common sense (Banister *et al.*, 1994). The behaviourist tradition in psychology which reduces language to forms of 'verbal behaviour' is unpalatable to many researchers today, not because it is empirically incorrect, which was the argument originally made against it inside psychology (Chomsky, 1959), but because it does not resonate with more cognitive and psychologized images of 'communication' that took hold in the discipline. Discourse Analysis focuses on language itself, and then language organized into higher-level forms of representation, which are then re-described within the terms of a particular approach (such as CA, EM or NA).

At the core of discourse analysis is a refusal of a 'humanist' conception of the human being as origin of meaning, and a refusal of methodologies that aim to search for such meanings (or intentions or cognitive mechanisms or emotions inside the mind of the speaker). A corresponding shift of perspective in research was developed in literary theory some years before in which the phrase 'death of the author' was used to capture the force of the argument (Barthes, 1967). Like literary theorists in the 'structuralist' and then 'post-structuralist' traditions of analysis, discourse analysts focus on the organization of a text, whether that is the text of an interview, newspaper article, novel or film for instance (Parker, 1992a). Let us turn to three kinds of connection that Thematic Analysis might make with other traditions of research.

First, TA can be articulated with an approach to discourse, and then could almost take form as a kind of 'discourse analysis' when it is used to accumulate and group a meaningful set of statements around a particular topic. For example, narratives may show commonalities across different speakers in a set of interviews, or there may be sets of metaphors used in a series of newspaper articles, or similar images used in advertising and film that can be treated as 'themes' (Reavey, 2011). Here the connection can be made with research in the 'social representations' tradition of research, in which there is the accumulation, grouping and interpretation of common motifs in a culture or subculture (Farr and Moscovici, 1984). The point has been made in that tradition of research that 'consensus' in the realm of representation is usually illusory, and this connects with an emphasis in discourse analysis on 'contradiction' (Rose *et al.*, 1995). In this respect, social representations, providing that they are interpretatively configured rather than seen as emerging from content analysis, can be treated as configurations of discourse.

When TA, in a second kind of connection, is articulated with 'Grounded Theory', however, the search for 'themes' becomes framed in ways closer to the empiricist tradition of research of psychology in the English-speaking world. Here, there is a claim that the researcher is actually 'discovering' the themes as underlying elements in the material, and that they are 'saturating' these themes and building a 'theory' only from the material that is analysed. Grounded Theory itself developed in US American sociology as a tactical methodological warrant for qualitative research, and it replicates many of the ground-rules of the quantitative tradition (Glaser and Strauss, 1967). Some kind of 'consensus' is then taken to mean that the analysis has been done well rather than, as we would suspect from a discourse-analytic perspective, badly. Motifs of 'discovery', scepticism about theoretical frameworks that might be mobilized to organize the material, and suspicion about the 'bias' introduced by the subjectivity of the researcher, are then compatible with mainstream psychology.

When TA is then, as a third option, articulated with 'Interpretative Phenomenological Analysis' the re-connection with a psychological way of understanding language is complete (Smith *et al.*, 2009). Here the claim is that the researcher, by putting aside their preconceptions (the ostensibly 'phenomenological' aspect of the approach) is able to access the meanings or 'themes' that underlie the accounts they gather (the apparently 'interpretative' aspect) and make them public (in what passes for the 'analysis'). Contradictions in this perspective would be treated as problems rather than, as they are in discourse analysis, resources. The search beneath what are taken to be surface meanings then leads the Thematic Analyst away from the contradictoriness of language, of discourse, to an illusory consistency at the level of their 'themes' (Parker, 2005a).

18 *Discourse analysis: dimensions of critique*

A critical-psychological appropriation of Thematic Analysis would tackle the key methodological question of 'selection' of material and of themes. It would take the first theoretically informed option – that which connects with social representations research – in order to show how psychological notions are historically constructed in different cultural or sub-cultural settings (Voelklein and Howarth, 2005). It would take care to avoid getting drawn into the psychologization of the research process (the idea that we are uncovering meanings in a text or speaker). Accounts of 'trauma', for example, can then be treated as one of a number of 'themes' or narratives about development that are culturally specific rather than being treated as universal phenomena (Levett, 1994).

The particular level of analysis inhabited by NA and TA, that of the individual life-story or the meaning of their experiences, thus poses methodological problems for discourse analysis. The move up a level, beyond 'interaction' as such, resolves some of these problems but poses other questions, which we turn to next.

Beyond interaction

We now move beyond the level of the individual to consider forms of discourse analysis that aim to bring into the equation study of socially structured power and ideological systems of meaning (Andersen, 1988). A shift of this kind was evident in the later work of some of those who introduced discourse analysis into social psychology (Wetherell and Potter, 1992). In these next two approaches, Critical Discourse Analysis and Foucauldian Discourse Analysis, the position of the researcher and the agency of the subject each become crucial to the way that questions are formulated and text is interpreted (Burman, 1992c). The methodological principles of an attention to history, theory and subjectivity, which are already important in the way we use the approaches we have already reviewed, are more obviously at stake in these kinds of research. It becomes clearer now, in addition, that 'discourse' is not confined to language at all, but includes all semiotically structured phenomena ranging from advertising images to the organization of space.

5 *In time: CDA*

The term 'critical' in Critical Discourse Analysis (CDA) carries with it a host of different meanings. According to some of its most enthusiastic advocates, the term is designed to signal some kind of affiliation to traditions of Marxist social theory, radical work in linguistics, and even recent developments in critical psychology (Van Dijk, 2003). After the very basic starting point that CDA is concerned with the way that power is enacted or resisted in discourse, however, there is little agreement about how exactly power should be conceptualized, and what methodologically would characterize it as a distinct approach. That is, there are no specific agreed theoretical foundations for CDA, even though the approach does usefully at least legitimize the use of theory as such.

This does not necessarily mean that the 'theory' will be radical in itself, and an accumulation of studies which show similarities across cultures of lexical and semantic markers of racism, for example, can simply end up as a warrant for a positivist theoretical stance on the world and what cannot be changed in it (Van Dijk, 2003). Some recent theoretical developments of what is called CDA has claimed allegiance to CA, and then to a quite explicitly cognitive theory that is grounded in an appeal to neurobiology, to the idea that the procedures discovered by CA in transcripts may also reveal hard-wired biological processes (Wodak and Chilton, 2005). This stance would then depart from any kind of 'critical psychology' that attends to the historical construction of interaction and psychological phenomena, that is, to the dimension of time in research.

In some cases, in such work carried out from within linguistics, the political position of the researcher is announced at the outset to provide the credentials for the discourse analysis to be understood to be critical (Fairclough, 1989). Here we see, in some way, allegiance to the idea that the position of the researcher is crucial to the process of gathering and interpreting 'data', if not also immediately to the idea that an attention to subjectivity should be built into the presentation of the work through a reflexive analysis (Finlay and Gough, 2003). In other cases, the political position of the researcher, and their 'critical' stance towards what they analyse is evident in the way the terms of the problem and the forms of analysis are elaborated as historical questions. This has led to the emergence of a sub-set of CDA as a self-styled 'Discourse Historical Analysis' (DHA), which raises a question as to whether the rest of CDA does or does not take history seriously enough, the implication being in the naming of DHA, that the rest of CDA does not (Wodak and Matouschek, 1993). A similar issue arises when there is a claim for a distinct 'Discourse Theoretical Analysis' (DTA), as if theory of some kind were absent from other work in CDA (Carpentier and De Cleen, 2007).

Either way, and whether or not DHA or DTA should be taken to be something different from CDA as such, this current of research does illustrate that a critical stance of any kind requires a theoretical and historical position to be taken by the researcher; a good example of this work examined how official communications to immigrants seeking naturalization in Austria contained certain words and phrases that resonated with the history of fascism in that country (Van Leeuwen and Wodak, 1999). To notice such semiotic links with the past, and to show why they are important today requires that the researcher goes beyond the text itself and uses their own cultural competence to make a political argument which challenges commonsensical meanings. This, rather than a restricted and empiricist focus on the text in CA, for example, is then seen as indicating good scholarship (Billig, 1988).

Studies that have claimed to draw upon CA and CDA in order to expose the way 'attention-deficit/hyperactivity disorder' (ADHD) constructs forms of pathology, for example, actually also show that once a 'critical' discursive stance is taken towards the material (there glossed as CDA), any specific form of description (there CA) is merely being mobilized for tactical purposes (McHoul and Rapley, 2005). This particular study of rival diagnostic methodologies employed by a doctor and parents of a child labelled with ADHD ends up (quite rightly) damning the diagnosis itself. This then has implications for the way psychology pathologizes those it claims to help, alerting us to the way that pathology is constructed in the positions that subjects may be assigned to even before they speak (Parker *et al.*, 1995).

Methodologically, the concern with 'coherence' in this kind of analysis is not so much because discourse itself should be seen as coherent, but because the story we tell about it has to be coherent to persuade others of the power discourse holds on its subjects (Hansen *et al.*, 2003). As we have already seen, this political stance, against abuse of power, which is essential to CDA, violates key tenets of CA as a methodologically pure technique. And, as with the case of Feminist Conversation Analysis, it is only when we are willing to take that step that we can do anything 'critical' or anything compatible with critical psychology.

6 In space: FDA

The next approach, Foucauldian Discourse Analysis (FDA), was constructed as a specific methodology inside psychology, and as an ally of a critical psychology (Alldred and Burman, 2005). This use of a distinctive current of social theory around the work of the historian and philosopher (and incidentally also one-time psychologist) Michel Foucault as a kind of method testifies to the way the discipline operates in line with what has been called the 'methodological imperative' in psychology (Danziger, 1985). This and the next two approaches we will consider are already 'critical', and what distinguishes them from each other are the specific theoretical frameworks they use, the way they conceptualize discourse even more than the way they suggest we, and researchers, read it (Sawyer, 2002).

Any approach which pretends to be 'Foucauldian' is also necessarily historical, to do with the time of phenomena, how they have come into being, how they maintain themselves and what forces may eventually lead to them disintegrating and disappearing altogether. Foucault (1966/1970) suggests that the figure of 'man' around which the 'human sciences' revolve may itself disappear, wiped away by the tides of time as if as a figure drawn in the sand. Discursive formations provide 'conditions of possibility' for reflection and elaboration of specific discourses which thereby host the statements which construct the objects of which we speak. Although Foucault (1980) invites us to use his work as a 'toolbox' to situate such discourses historically, the closest he actually comes to a theoretical system to grasp their nature today is one which is concerned with the organization of space rather than time.

Writing against a linear developmental history of the emergence of disciplines like psychology, Foucault emphasizes the way that forms of power operate to organize and regulate space, to observe and discipline those who inhabit particular positions within it (Hook, 2007). We thus also return to the debate over humanism and 'anti-humanism', but now with an attention to the way that humanism operates to recruit subjects so that they will speak willingly to experts about themselves; 'anti-humanism' here operates as a more radical theoretical account of the forms of agency that might resist this peculiarly modern exercise of power.

FDA adapted this theoretical-historical account of power and discourse to a deliberately radical challenge to ideology in psychology (Willig, 2001), even though Foucault himself was sceptical about the term 'ideology' because it discursively seemed to presuppose that there was, underneath, a truth that it obscured. The crystallization of the approach into FDA – into steps and stages and suchlike – was then a tactical discourse-analytic move to draw attention to the intimate link between discourse and power (Arribas-Ayllon and Walkerdine, 2008).

Some other currents within discourse analysis concerned with ideology and power can also be grouped here with FDA even if they do not share the specific historical analysis Foucault provided in his earlier work. Studies of the way that ideology works by setting up a series of 'dilemmas' through which speakers discursively anticipate objections to what they are saying (Billig *et al.*, 1988), and of the way that 'positions' are constructed in discourse so that speakers are boxed in to certain kinds of response to power (Davies and Harré, 1990) owe something to Foucault's approach to discourse, if only to the idea that knowledge is linked to power, and that this knowledge is contradictory, that power is intertwined with resistance (Foucault, 1977). What is understood to be 'pathology' at one moment, then, can be turned back on power as a 'counter-discourse' (Burman *et al.*, 1996).

Insofar as critical psychology refuses any particular psychological model of the person as the grounds of its own critique of the discipline, it is effectively Foucauldian, and pathologizing terms such as 'psychotic' would always be turned back upon systems of power to ask in what ways the discourses that label others are themselves 'psychotic discourses', for example (Hook and Parker, 2002). This form of discourse analysis is always searching for points of conflict, something more visceral and subversive than mere methodological concern with 'contradiction'.

Production of analytic phenomena

The final two approaches we will consider could be viewed as in some way 'post-Foucauldian' in that they build upon some of the premises of the CDA and FDA work, but introduce specific theoretical concepts. Rather than being seen as taking us up to another level higher than the historical and spatial operations of power we explore in CDA and FDA, it would perhaps be more accurate to say that these next two approaches raise questions about how we conceptualize the process of reading discourse as if from the 'outside' and in relation to politics. The first of these approaches, Semiotic Analysis, does presuppose some specific theoretical coordinates to make sense of subjectivity in language and image, and the second approach, Political Discourse Theory gives a little more room to question those coordinates.

7 In time: SA

Most approaches to discourse analysis would include in the broad scope of 'discourse' language as such and also images that are, we could say, structured like a language and can be read as such. New 'visual methodologies' in psychology have drawn on discourse-analytic ideas to examine how images are structured and how they might be interpreted (Reavey, 2011). From outside psychology in the field of cultural studies, an approach which we can for shorthand purposes term 'Semiotic Analysis' (SA) emerged to 'decode' images (Chandler, 2007), and it also draws explicitly or implicitly on psychoanalytic notions of subjectivity and the production of subject positions for readers of texts.

This semiotic approach is not confined to images, however, and it has methodological implications for how we then read written texts as well. Semiotics was first proposed as a 'science of signs' as the foundation of what became known as structural linguistics, and it inaugurated a tradition of research, structuralism and 'post-structuralism', that is usually taken to include Foucault, for example, and the psychoanalyst Jacques Lacan (Sarup, 1988). A combination of theorists from this tradition was brought to bear on psychology in some influential critiques just before discourse analysis appeared as a full-blown methodological alternative (Henriques *et al.*, 1998). Analysis of advertisements is a fitting place to begin, for one of the premises of Semiotic Analysis is that images are organized into forms of discourse that also advertise, that sell us images of ourselves to which we have to some extent conform in order to be able to read them. Advertising exaggerates everyday commonsensical forms of life – of gender, for example – in its representations in order to work, and when read critically provides an opportunity to see the dominant ideology at work (Goffman, 1979).

In order to 'decode' advertisements, there needs to be description of the way that ideological material is configured for subjects to read it as being for them, for the kind of subjects they are (Williamson, 1978). There is, then, a temporal process at work in advertising, in the ideological structure and effect of advertising, through which a subject comes to recognize how they are being addressed in order to solve a puzzle that is set up in the images and then to find that sense of who they are confirmed as they are able to make sense of it and their place within it.

At the heart of this process is a little narrative which SA borrows from the structuralist political theorist Louis Althusser to describe this address to subjects as 'interpellation'. When a policeman calls out to a subject, they recognize themselves as subject of that hailing or interpellation as good citizen or criminal, in a specific constellation of relations to the state and ideology (Althusser, 1970/1971). In the same way, images call out to subjects.

The researcher therefore needs to be able to draw upon their own subjective responses, their own responses to being 'hailed' by the images, and then, as a methodological imperative in this kind of work, they need to craft an account that is meaningful to those who will read the study. This 'crafting' must successfully interpellate the reader of the analysis, must draw them into the account so it is credible to them.

This account of interpellation relies on psychoanalysis, at least on the idea that a subject is called into place at some unconscious level rather than at a conscious or cognitive level (Dashtipour, 2012). Recent Lacanian Discourse Analysis (LDA) (Pavón Cuéllar, 2010) has attempted to develop an analysis that does not burrow underneath language, or inject interpretations into the text (as Thematic Analysis or Kleinian 'free associative narrative inquiry' approaches tend to do) (Parker, 2005a).

There are two key issues here. The first is to do with the relation between language and the unconscious in psychoanalysis, and Lacan's argument that language is a precondition for the unconscious as a historically constituted phenomenon (Archard, 1984). The second is to do with time, and with an attempt to break out of the rather static picture of ideology and interpellation presented by Althusser as a philosopher of order who does not anticipate change in discourse (Ranciere, 1974/2011).

The next step in LDA is to show how discursive 'conditions of possibility' (to put it in Foucauldian terms) are also conditions of possibility for what Lacan called an 'act' or what the Lacanian post-Althusserian political theorist Alain Badiou (2005) calls an 'event'. An emphasis on the indeterminacy of language in Lacanian Discourse Analysis allows for a connection with the subversive radical tradition in critical psychology that wants to change the world rather than simply interpret it (Parker and Pavón Cuéllar, 2013). From a critical psychology perspective, however, we would also need to take care to see psychoanalysis itself, including Lacanian psychoanalysis, as a historically constituted system of theory and practice rather than universal truth about the human subject (Parker, 2011b).

8 In space: PDT

Political Discourse Theory (PDT) brings to these debates a series of concepts that are elaborated from structural linguistics and an explicit engagement with political debate on the Left in the work of Ernesto Laclau and Chantal Mouffe. These interventions have run alongside the development of discourse analysis inside psychology but have rarely connected with it, and they also provide some of the earliest discourse-analytic uses of psychoanalysis. Some strands of CDA did also attempt to integrate Marx and Freud in the early years (Hodge and Kress, 1988), an attempt that is now completely obscured by the 'cognitive' turn in CDA. Laclau and Mouffe were responsible for the introduction of Slavoj Žižek (1990) into British social theory debates in the late 1980s, and they have been pressed more recently by some of their former students to make their use of Lacanian psychoanalytic ideas more explicit (Stavrakakis, 2007).

A complete structured alternative political-theoretical system has been elaborated from inside the PDT tradition (Glynos and Howarth, 2007) which builds on an account of the 'logic of fantasy' to explain why forms of discourse have such a strong grip on its subjects (Glynos, 2001). The elaboration of ideological material through which texts re-present the world for its subjects in PDT is organized around a structural-linguistic account of 'signifiers', discrete elements of discourse that may take the form of words, phrases or images. A text is held in place by certain key, 'master signifiers' which anchor meaning for subjects. Certain kinds of signifiers can be identified which stand in for the fantasy that the system of language in a community can be completed or filled in, to signify the impossible fullness of society – these are the 'empty signifiers' like 'democracy' or 'happiness' or 'self-fulfilment' – and other signifiers are identified over which there is a struggle by different groups to define; these signifiers are 'floating signifiers' like 'nation' or 'race' or 'gender' (Howarth *et al.*, 2000). The struggle over signification in the space of a particular culture is a struggle for 'hegemony', an ideological battle which discourse analysis participates in when it interprets text (Laclau and Mouffe, 1985).

This is a quite specific account of the operation of master, empty and floating signifiers in discourse, but PDT also connects with feminist and queer theory interventions which focus on the way that discourse 'performs' and 'reiterates' dominant forms of identity, and the way indeterminacy of meaning gives space for subjects to redefine themselves (Butler *et al.*, 2000). The work of Judith Butler (1997), for example, is not usually seen as a kind of 'discourse analysis', but it is concerned with the same kind of activity of interpreting, questioning and reconfiguring language, and has been a direct inspiration for forms of critical psychology, feminist psychology and critical discursive psychology (Burman, 2010).

It was one of the commonplaces of right-wing political discourse in Britain in the 1980s that, in Margaret Thatcher's words, 'there is no such thing as society' (Parker, 1989). PDT is as suspicious of the construct 'society', and has been criticized for apparently turning discourse as such into an overarching ontological and epistemological force that overrides materialist accounts of political-economic conditions in which discourse functions (Geras, 1987). Early advocates of discourse theory had argued that language itself was a material force, and analysis of it could be thought of as 'materialist' (Coward and Ellis, 1977). PDT never bought the other aspect of Thatcher's statement, that 'there are only individual men and women and families', because the 'social constructionist' impulse of PDT (to borrow a term from critical-psychological debates inside the discipline) has entailed a questioning of the category of the 'individual', of 'men' and 'women' and 'families' too (Burman, 2008b).

All forms of 'identity', including every construct assumed to be self-identical in psychological discourse, is open to question in PDT. In this respect it chimes with the social constructionist argument in the discipline that it is not then the case that 'anything goes', a politically irresponsible simple relativism, but that 'nothing goes' (Stainton Rogers *et al.*, 1995). Every form of discourse about the social and about individuals is interrogated by discourse analysis, or by other forms of critical methodology which require that the 'stance' of the researcher is brought into play.

Critical issues

These eight different approaches to discourse analysis provide concepts that can be taken up by a researcher in order to build their own 'methodology' suited to the questions they want to ask (Burman and Parker, 1993). There are some remaining critical issues that need to be addressed, however.

The first set of issues concern the nature of 'subjectivity' and the way it may be used as a methodological resource that either conforms to or challenges the forms of subjectivity that are assumed to operate in discourse itself. Subjectivity not only changes over time, a question of history, but that change is mediated by quite specific forms of discourse. For example, it has been argued from within CDA that new forms of interaction in cyberspace give rise to new forms of subjectivity that then require new forms of analysis (Chouliaraki and Fairclough, 2000). The relation between what is taken to be 'inside' the subject and what is 'outside' then may be changing. This opens up new questions about the nature of 'affect' in psychology which break completely from modern psychology to what is sometimes seen as a 'non-foundational' kind of work (Brown and Stenner, 2009).

This means that discourse analysis needs to attend to the way assumptions about the nature of language and subjectivity from mainstream discourse themselves enter into the research process. Instead of 'emotion' being seen as inside the individual driving or disrupting discourse, for example, it can be treated as one of the effects of a certain kind of 'territorialization' of affect, and a quite different conception of what 'ethics' is in psychology (Neill, 2015). Cognitive or mainstream psychoanalytic models of the subject that thrive inside psychology or compete with it as an alternative kind of 'psychology' are then inadequate to the theoretical and historical work that is necessary for discourse analysis (Hook, 2011).

We then need to turn around and ask from what 'position' we carry out research. Standard approaches to reflexivity in qualitative research in psychology invite the researcher to speak about their 'journey' into the research, and this can then give a rather confessional tenor to the account, something that Foucault (1976/1981) would have recognized as part of the regulation of subjectivity in modern Western culture. When we critical psychologists refer to 'position' in reflexivity, however, we should be focusing on the institutional framing of research questions, and the way that our objects of study are configured by us as subjects who are willing to speak to the experts, to those wanting to gather information about 'life outside' the academic institutions (Parker, 2005a).

The activity of the discourse analyst must then be situated in the wider landscape of psychologization in Western culture, one which agonizes about the responsibility of the academics to reflect on what they do and subjects the analyst as much to psychological forms of reasoning as their objects living in what researchers think of as the real world (De Vos, 2012). Discourse analysis could then be treated as one of the signs of psychologization, as what was hitherto assumed to be most intimate to the human subject, their speech, is interrogated and the language itself is picked apart as if it was itself the site of subjectivity (Cameron, 1995).

Discourse analysis was, at one moment, seen as synonymous with critical psychology in the discipline, but it has succeeded in showing itself to be useful to the discipline, and critical psychologists now need to trace how the approach has been recuperated by the institutions it thought it could subvert (Parker, 2012). 'Critique' can itself then become discursively absorbed by psychology as an indication that the researcher is a flexible, adaptive subject open to change and new challenges that face psychology as it adapts itself to neoliberalism, to the deregulation of the old disciplines. This account of discourse analysis is one account, and a critical-psychological reflexive move would now be to ask, at the very least, what kind of discourse this discourse reproduces, and what positions we could take towards it that challenge rather than confirm the power of academic institutions today.

2 Four story-theories about and against postmodernism in psychology

> One conceptual issue that dogged discourse analysis as it started to make itself at home in psychology was the question as to whether the 'turn to discourse' amounted to the development of a 'postmodern' psychology. The old paradigm was certainly quite 'modernist' in the sense that it adhered to notions of scientific understanding, rational enlightenment and progress. The new paradigm 'turn to language' also seemed to follow that spirit of research in psychology.
>
> This chapter, originally published in a US book on 'postmodern psychologies', locates the development of discourse analysis, a 'turn to discourse', in relation to a social constructionist and postmodern turn in the social sciences. Discourse analysis does seem to treat psychology as no more than a collection of stories, and this pluralist relativism could be seen as postmodern.
>
> The chapter takes up arguments within contemporary critical psychology about the nature of scientific paradigms, culture, reality and experience, and I use four 'story-theories' to frame these issues: first, an exploration of how postmodern ideas have given shape to the way some critical psychologists have attempted to move the 'paradigm shifts' in psychology forward; second, an attempt to connect these ideas with a broader view of the state of psychology in capitalist society; third, a review of the implications of the postmodern turn in psychology and in other disciplines for our understanding of the real world; and fourth, a reflection on the way postmodern psychologists might be tempted to dissolve critical psychology into therapy. The line running through the dis-

> cussion of postmodern psychology in these story-theories, and
> summarized in the concluding section of the chapter, is that critical psychologists sceptical about postmodernism should use it
> but tactically. We do not need to buy into postmodernism to keep
> struggling against the still dominant modern psychology.

Why four 'story-theories'? In February 1997 the front page of a liberal-left British daily newspaper, *The Guardian*, presented four different explanations of confusion over whether the lead singer with Manchester band Oasis, Liam Gallagher, was actually going to marry his girlfriend, Patsy Kensit, or not. The press, mainstream and tabloid, had been obsessed with rumours of the wedding for over a week, and now it was time to ask 'What's the story?' The first explanation canvassed in the article was 'The postmodern story theory':

> This posits that Liam and Patsy are locked into a post-ironic symbiosis with a [sic] increasingly marketized media, where there is a continuum between truth and untruth and between the exploiter and exploited. Under this theory, there never was going to be a wedding, but it suited both band and media to play along with the construct
>
> (*The Guardian*, 11 February 1997)

The other possibilities reviewed were 'The naked commercialism story theory' (to distract attention from a new album release by Oasis arch-rivals, the Essex-based band Blur), 'The extremely unlikely story theory' (that the wedding had been called off because of media attention), and the '"Don't know what the story is, but we've all been had again" theory' (as a replay of music press hype over a possible band split between Liam and Noel, his brother, the previous September).

There is a double-movement going on here between form and content, between the *structure* of the narrative that is used to tell us four stories about the wedding and the *topic* which is reframed four times over. At the same time as this structural fragmentation occurs, something happens to the topic such that we fail to learn anything more about it. Here the postmodern story theory wins out overall. All that we can know is that we can know many different things. So, something *serious* is happening to our mode of understanding, our structuring of the phenomenon, at the very moment that the process *trivializes* what we are trying to understand, the topic. Because this example is only about Oasis, trivializing the topic more than it has been already does not really matter much, but when we turn to the discipline of psychology it really does matter *how* we trivialize it, *why* we do it and *when* we move into a serious reflection on what we are doing. I will trace my way through these issues using headings from those media speculations about Liam and Patsy, so we start with the postmodern story theory.

The postmodern story theory

The last thirty years have seen an increasing interest in 'social constructionist' perspectives in psychology in general (Gergen, 1985), and in approaches which locate the stuff of psychology in discourse in particular (Burr, 2003). This movement represents a critical reflexive shift away from the search for mental paraphernalia inside each individual's head and towards a socially mediated and historically situated study of action and experience. This is an endeavour postmodernism both encourages and sabotages.

The 'new paradigm' turn to language in the 1970s encouraged a challenge to traditional laboratory-experimental psychology (Harré and Secord, 1972). Criticisms of laboratory-experimentation in psychology at the end of the 1960s were fired by anger at the deceptive and demeaning practices that underpinned the discipline, and humanist arguments were often more important then than 'scientific' ones. There were attempts to balance humanism and science, for example, in the slogan 'for scientific purposes treat people as if they were human beings' (Harré and Secord, 1972: 84). Despite this clear bid to be a new scientific paradigm for psychology, scientific rhetoric soon dropped into the background, and it was as a *relativizing* (if not yet fully relativist) current of work that the new paradigm arguments quickly spread from social psychology (Harré, 1979) to studies of the self (Harré, 1983; Shotter, 1984), emotion (Harré, 1986b) and cognitive psychology (Edwards, 1997; Harré and Gillett, 1994). Social constructionist and discourse-analytic approaches made it possible to conceptualize human psychology as something culturally located and historically specific, and they have even served as a warrant for renewed discussion of Marxist accounts of the individual subject as an 'ensemble of social relations' (Parker and Spears, 1996).

'Postmodern psychology' is the latest rubric, then, for the critical and then 'deconstructive' line of work which spread from social psychology through to other areas of the discipline from the 1970s through to the end of the 1980s (Kvale, 1992). But as it turned postmodern it started to pose problems for those critical psychologists who were trying to combat 'modern' psychology without being trapped into something which served as its equally apolitical mirror image. Although a collection of critical essays in social psychology published in 1974 was entitled *Reconstructing Social*

Psychology (Armistead, 1974) and a follow-up some fifteen years later was called *Deconstructing Social Psychology* (Parker and Shotter, 1990), little of substance in the complaints and political impulse had changed. Concerns about the political passivity of a politics of 'deconstruction' for feminists were included in the latter book (Burman, 1990), but this has not hindered the application of 'deconstruction' to other topics in psychology (e.g. Burman, 1994; Parker *et al.*, 1995).

Postmodernism and power

Some of the dangers of full-blown relativism that mars much recent postmodern psychology can already be seen in the rhetoric of the earlier days of the new paradigm. It will be clearer what the consequences of this rhetoric are if we consider social constructionist accounts of power. One of the influential alternative theoretical 'new paradigm' traditions in psychology during the 1970s was 'ethogenic' social psychology, in which close observation of the roles people adopted in different situations and the rules they followed was combined with gathering 'accounts' from people about those roles and rules (Harré and Secord, 1972; Marsh *et al.*, 1974). Notwithstanding Harré's (1986a) own sustained argument for realism in the sciences, he then argued that power is 'an ontological illusion, real only as an accounting resource' (Harré, 1979: 233). This claim would not necessarily be problematic if it were supplemented by an analysis of the way 'accounting resources' are structured so as to distribute power and perform it in the exercise of knowledge, for example, but Harré is insistent that social systems which appear to be structured around power are 'nothing above the multiplication of personal power' (ibid.). Any 'account' we may want to give of power in society or the state, then, is levelled down to one of many 'accounts' that any of the other players may be offering. This example is so telling precisely because it comes from someone who is a realist who then makes use of social constructionism and then, perhaps, regrets its effects (Harré, 1992, 1995).

Postmodern psychology and 'deconstruction' in psychology have included writers who want to understand and challenge power, but bit by bit psychologists who should know better have succumbed to the apolitical impulse of postmodernism. The emergence of a version of 'discourse analysis' in social psychology towards the end of the 1980s (Potter and Wetherell, 1987) was given the tag quote (from Ken Gergen) in publishers publicity of being a 'postmodern psychology'. This hope for something entirely new has set the scene for a discourse of critique that has continued apace ever since. The fragmentation of what we know about Liam and Patsy into the four different versions works rather like a discourse analysis, and in that respect it makes sense to view discourse analysis in psychology as a postmodern story. However, we can get a better sense of why new paradigm and then postmodern hopes in psychology sold us short with respect to issues of power only if we turn to the wider societal context. To do this, we need the naked commercialism story theory.

The naked commercialism story theory

The variety of critical movements relativizing alienating and oppressive psychological knowledge about people have usually been characterized by an insistence that the 'individual' and the 'social' were so interrelated that a strict distinction between the two sides of the equation was seriously mistaken. The argument that psychology *is* social (e.g. Armistead, 1974) was an influential theme in early critical perspectives, and it continues today (e.g. Gergen, 1994). Critics also often pointed out that attempts in 'social' psychology to specify *how* the individual and the social were connected reproduced the self-same dualist problematic (Buss, 1975; Henriques *et al.*, 1998). This is where descriptions of 'dialectical' relationships started to appear, particularly in developmental psychology, where dialectics was employed as part of an account of the way in which an 'individual' child emerged out of the relationship between infant and mother (e.g. Riegel, 1976). Psychology, like other bourgeois disciplines, however, has been adept at absorbing and neutralizing Marxist concepts. And, just as 'alienation' has been redefined as an individual feeling of worthlessness rather than an account of the real separation of people from their labour (e.g. Seeman, 1971), so the term 'dialectics' is often used in psychology simply to describe the balance between the individual and the social, between inside and outside or between objectivity and subjectivity.

The latest 'postmodern' version of this domestication of dialectics in psychology can be seen in 'deconstruction'. Just as modern psychology succeeded in destroying what was genuinely radical about dialectics, now postmodern psychology is doing the same job for the discipline on deconstruction. The argument that deconstruction in psychology ought to emphasize undecidability, and that the moral of Derrida's work is that we should perpetually defer a judgement about what may or may not be the case or what may or may not be right or wrong (e.g. Hepburn, 1999) is of a piece with the rhetorical balancing so beloved of bourgeois culture. This version of deconstruction, which is deliberately counterposed to approaches in psychology which attend to the power and politics of the psy-complex (e.g. Burman, 1994; Parker *et al.*, 1995), is closer to the US liberal pluralist readings of Derrida's work than the progressive uses of deconstruction in literary theory in Europe (Norris, 1996). While this rhetorical balancing strategy presents itself as being the most open inclusive defence of conversation about how the world may be, then, it is actually very selective about which theoretical traditions are included and about which readings of theories will be allowed.

Against this postmodern relativism, we should be sympathetic at this point to those 'critical relativists' who refuse to brook *any* attempt to resort to science in psychology, whether to improve or challenge it. For the radical textualists in the discipline who analyse the way 'development' and 'emotions' are 'storied' into being (e.g. Curt, 1994; Stainton Rogers *et al.*, 1995), an embrace of old modern 'realist' psychology is also a dangerous invitation to critical psychologists to be seduced back into the discipline and to join in the enterprise of demarcating the 'mere' story from the 'real' psychology (and so to carry on with all the more arrogance than before). The 'critical relativist' position, then, entails

> a social constructionism whereby people are viewed as readers and writers (written upon and read) within the Textuality of culture. People (and this includes people who are psychologists/social scientists) actively construct (and are actively constructed by) versions of the 'way things are', versions which are always-already enmeshed with the moral, political and ideological concerns of Being.
> (Stenner and Eccleston, 1994: 96)

Postmodernism and ideology

Postmodernism appears in psychology in at least *three* different versions, in which it sells itself to those jaded with the old paradigm as living in the story worlds of 'Opportunity', 'Progress' and 'Reflection' (Parker, 1998a). Lyotard (1979/1984), one of the key theoreticians of the 'postmodern condition', can be recruited to each of these market segments, and he even can seem compatible to the reflexive 'critical relativist' argument. What Lyotard does, however, is to try and strip the modern and the postmodern of its insistent movement forward, of the anticipatory dynamic of modernism. The futurism of modern experimental art, for example, is overshadowed by a reflection on narrative as something which is only in the present and from which there is no escape, back or forward;

> What seems to be moving in such moments is less 'history' than that which is unleashed by its rupture and suspension; and the typically modernist images of the vortex and the abyss, 'vertical' inruptions into temporality within which forces swirl restlessly in an eclipse of linear time, represent this ambivalent consciousness.
> (Eagleton, 1985: 67)

Postmodernism in the story-world of Reflection is part of a world which values that restlessness and sees it as an always already present quality of modern experience. This vision of the postmodern condition as consisting of 'games of perfect information at any given moment' leads Lyotard (1979/1984: 67) to hope that it would furnish 'a politics that would respect both the desire for justice and the desire for the unknown'. It is a moot point as to whether postmodern ideas offer anything generally to those in the real world. What is for sure is that when psychologists get hold of postmodernism they tend to turn it into an ideology which celebrates the way things are instead of providing any way out.

Postmodernism, psychology and capitalism

Psychology has always traded in ideological representations of mind and behaviour, so it is hardly surprising that postmodern psychologists should carry on that tradition. But the relationship between modernity and ideology, and between postmodernism and psychology is complex and contradictory. Postmodern psychology encourages individuals to subvert and surpass the rules of the game laid down by the discipline. But even as we should give credit to these critical writers, we need to be careful not to overestimate what they can achieve, for two reasons.

First, psychology has continually failed to fix behaviour and mental mechanisms as it would wish and it has been repeatedly challenged by writers who have explicitly wanted to improve it and turn it around to the cause of resistance and liberation. The psy-complex, as a dense network of theories and practices inside and outside the academe and the clinic, is a dangerous and pernicious regulative apparatus, but it still fails. Its subjects look for holistic alternatives that will respect their experience and acknowledge diversity, and the reductive and reified models it peddles are often, quite rightly, treated with contempt. Some people are impressed by psychology, and those who are training to be psychologists and hoping for a share of the power are most susceptible, but fortunately many people are suspicious of psy-complex apparatchiks and mocking of those who speak its language. They have not needed postmodernism so far to help them resist psychology. Postmodern writing does draw attention to the way 'modern' psychology caricatures notions of historical progress and represses self-understanding, but it then itself paralyses and ironizes our grasp of history and agency in return. It is, then, a liability for those who have always already struggled against the discipline with an eye to history and agency.

Second, postmodernism is itself, of course, a kind of conceptual commodity in a world still defined by parameters of progress, reflection and opportunity. It has to be marketed to audiences who weigh up whether it will help them to move forward and whether it will facilitate self-understanding. However, although critical psychologists are sickened by the way psychology fails them – the way it takes the hope of historical progress and makes a caricature of it in the steady accumulation of facts from discrete controlled variables, and systematically represses self-understanding because it threatens to introduce a spiral of subjectivity into its supposedly objective studies – some of them are still reluctant to buy postmodernism (e.g. Roiser, 1997). They are right. As we have already seen, postmodernism relativizes our accounts of the world to such an extent that we cannot then produce a critical understanding of the social and economic conditions which produce the kind of oppressive practices and ideas psychology routinely trades in. We can see how extremely unlikely and pernicious the postmodern story is if we look at how it corrodes realist accounts outside psychology.

The extremely unlikely story theory

Postmodern relativism provokes irrational conspiratorial views of the world, mystifies our understanding of state power and undermines historical narrative. To say the story postmodernism tells is 'extremely unlikely' is the least of it. Conspiracy theory and mystification in the place of social analysis and reasoned argument abounds in 'postmodern' sectors of contemporary culture. One trivial example is discussions on the internet in the late 1990s about the connections in the narrative of the film *The Wizard of Oz* and the Pink Floyd album *Dark Side of the Moon* – in which, for example, the Tin Man in the film reveals that he does not have a heart at exactly the same point in the album where the heartbeat appears. Another serious example is Baudrillard's (1995) claim that the Gulf War in the Iraq did not *really* happen. Such a claim plays a profoundly ideological role. Postmodern celebration of irrationality and mystification also has disastrous consequences for the past and the present, and historical revisionists are all too ready to jump on the postmodern bandwagon to erase the past (cf. Norris, 1996). Remember Walter Benjamin's (1939: 247) warning: 'Only that historian will have the gift of fanning the spark of hope in the past who is firmly convinced that *even the dead* will not be safe from the enemy if he wins'. The theoretical resources that relativist researchers draw upon are part of a wider discursive turn in the human sciences that carry conservative as well as progressive prescriptions for social activity (Callinicos, 1995; Eagleton, 1991; Geras, 1995; Norris, 1996). Critical psychologists – relativist and realist – have expressed concern about this, but attempts to address the issue have tended to illustrate and explore the problem rather than clarify and resolve it (e.g. Parker, 1998b). There is, however, always room for hope, for notwithstanding the naive or malign excesses of the Baudrillards and the historical revisionists, relativist arguments are untenable. They break down because we, and those who make such arguments, do still live in the real world.

Postmodernism and the real world

We all, at times, make realist assumptions about the world, and it would not be possible for us to discuss alternative accounts if we did not; 'conversation as between separate intelligences itself presupposes a structured and differentiated segment of public "matter" between them, independently of their jointly finding or deciding or agreeing that it is so structured and differentiated' (Geras, 1995: 118). Even those in the relativist camp will display due caution about denying the existence of a world, and they are eventually compelled take back most of their untenable anti-realist claims. This is why a little textual analysis will reveal a rhetorical balance between extravagance and caution in the very same arguments advanced by 'postmodern' writers like Rorty (e.g. 1989, 1992). There is always a rhetorical balancing act in the arguments of 'relativists' in which they take back many of the extreme claims they make, almost in the same breath. A close examination of Rorty's writing, for example, reveals that theoretical claims about pragmatism are always balanced by a recognition that it could not really be defended it were taken to the limit (Geras, 1995).

While Rorty's writing is characterized by an extravagant relativism, this is always moderated by assurances that 'of course' this or that shared knowledge that we have about the world can be taken for granted and will *not* be subjected to scrutiny; this is because 'He cannot cope with explaining how, if there is not something which is what it is apart from any description, there could be something which pre-existed all description; as to the best of our knowledge there is' (Geras, 1995: 132). There must be a 'real' social world that we share in order to be able to make sense of Rorty's argument, and so,

> Like most people, Rorty needs some terms for the brute facticity of things, if he cannot have this coherently, then incoherently it must be. For without it he cannot cope. He cannot cope with the overwhelming paradox and absurdity which will follow upon losing the world
>
> (ibid.)

Often, however, what stems this relativism, and grounds the claims in something we can recognize as 'real', are different rhetorical devices that assure the reader that they live in the same world as Rorty. In the process, these devices draw the reader into the text so that the world they inhabit with him while they read it is suffused with ideology. One grounding device, for example, is the appeal to the audience as members of a common culture, a covert nationalist rhetoric which, in Rorty's writing, makes the United States appear in the text as the home of liberal democracy (Billig, 1993).

Rorty is one of the postmoderns who resorts to the argument that they are not so much anti-realist as 'anti-representationalists'; 'Like Berkeley and Kant . . . contemporary anti-representationalists insist that they do not deny the prior and independent reality of the referents of many beliefs' (Rorty, 1992: 41). In a riposte to Eagleton's (1991) discussion of ideology, Rorty (1992: 41) agrees with the attempt to discover alternative accounts of a situation that a Marxist may see as 'oppressive', in this case in an analysis of the interests of a galley slave who may realize later that the life they were leading was buttressed by forms of discourse which misrepresented their true interests; 'Anti-representationalists can happily agree with Eagleton that when the galley slave thought he was a justly lashed worm, he was wrong, and that he is now right in thinking that his interests consist in escaping the galleys'. However, ideology as such is dissolved as a category, and there is no way that the analysis of the slave's situation could be construed as *actually really* oppressive. For Rorty, what the slave does when they speak about their situation differently is to reconfigure their relationship to the experience; so the 'anti-representationalist' 'will also construe this claim as saying: if the slave tries the discourse of emancipation he will come out with better results than those he achieved with the discourse in which he viewed himself as a worm' (Rorty, 1992: 41).

Postmodernism and modern psychology

How does this play itself out with respect to *psychology*? Here we have to be very careful, for realism as such may not be so much an antidote to postmodernism as something that leads back to modern psychology. Realism in psychology has rested on the argument that human beings should be respected as structured entities which engage in 'second-order monitoring' (Harré and Secord, 1972). This reflexive power of human beings means that a watertight 'closed system' which (nearly) obtains in the natural sciences could not apply in psychology, save by the most brutal suppression of reflexivity and so the destruction of human psychology itself. Psychology was seen by Harré and Secord (1972) as one level in an open system of structures that was embedded in biological structures and social structures. They argued that psychological matters are of moral-political concern, as with other sciences, but in this discipline all the more so because the forms of knowledge that psychology produces are deployed by its very objects of study. Psychology cannot accurately 'represent' psychological functioning because, as a shared system of knowledge, it is part of it. However, patterns can be identified to model already existing but mutable structures which permit and constrain behaviour and the accounts people may give of it.

While these arguments cut against 'old paradigm' psychology they do not in themselves serve as a critical counterweight to the dangerous aspects of postmodern psychology. Postmodern psychology refuses to take seriously accounts of the real world – the world in which the discipline of psychology causes so much harm – so why should it take seriously realism (or 'critical realism') in psychology when it claims to study 'real' psychological processes. This refusal by the postmoderns is actually a mixed blessing for critical psychologists, for many of us have been trying to refuse the reification of things psychologists think they have 'discovered' as real things for years. For critical psychologists who do want to develop their work in the context of an understanding of ideology and power in the real world, the realist ratification of psychology is dangerous. Postmodernism is sometimes attractive to critical psychologists precisely because critical realists outside psychology do often threaten to buttress *modern* psychology. Postmodernism then seems the only way out. Collier (1994), for example, argues that while he does not hope for a 'critical realist psychology' (quite rightly), he then lets existing theories in psychology (such as Chomsky's) off the hook by suggesting that already established theories might be challenged or refined by critical realists (Collier, 1994: 207). This is why some critical psychologists sometimes play with postmodern and relativist ideas *inside* the discipline of psychology while using realist (and necessarily antipostmodern) ideas to contextualize what the discipline does on the *outside* (Parker, 1999a). Critical psychologists are trying to avoid being duped into assumptions about human beings made by psychologists, *modern or postmodern*. They insist that they do not know what the story is about fixed human nature, thinking or behaviour, and they do not want to be had again by any theory which lures them into thinking they should know (cf. Newman and Holzman, 1997).

'Don't know what the story is, but we've all been had again' theory

Postmodernism is very appealing to critical psychologists because it manifests itself as a 'psychological' phenomenon, appearing in everyday experience as an expression of present-day uncertainties about identity and meaning, and because it is marked self-consciously and self-referentially in contemporary culture. We can see the experiential aspect of postmodernism in the following two dreams reported by colleagues a few years back. One of the dreamers is a woman, a teacher and psychotherapist. The second dreamer is a man, a clinical psychologist.

The first dream. She is wending her way up and around the contours of a mountain range. She is passing hedges and hillocks and stones as she makes her way up to the top. She reaches the top of one of the higher hills, and realizes that it is in the shape of a letter. As she looks across the pattern of hills below her she realizes, and she feels anxious as she realizes, that it is one of a series of letters that together spell out the word 'postmodernism'. She wakes up.

The second dream. He discovers that one of his legs is made of metal. It is a false leg. He knows, as he looks down at his flesh and blood leg on one side and at his metal leg on the other, that one of his legs is modern and the other is postmodern. He knows which is which, but he also knows, when he awakes, that others may not know. When he does wake up, he describes the dream to friends, and asks each of them if they know which leg is which.

These dreams display an attempt, in the first dream, to find meaning in nature and, in the second dream, to determine the meaning of bits of the body. There is a concern in both with individual identity and with how it might be located. To see the word 'postmodernism' written over nature is at least to be aware of culture as a construction, and to puzzle over real and false bits of the body is at least to ask what is what. Such themes in contemporary culture also, of course, serve as an invitation to therapy. Therapy operates as a domain in which critical reflection all too often turns into decontextualized 'reflexivity' and this reflexivity is then often viewed as equivalent to a postmodern psychology.

Postmodernism and reflexivity

One of the symptoms of therapeutic discourse in psychology is that there is often a simple appeal to 'reflexivity' to solve problems of politics and power in the discipline. Some writers in the tradition of discourse analysis also appeal to reflexivity even though they are otherwise extremely suspicious of anything that looks therapeutic, to the extent that talk of subjectivity of any sort is accused by them of slipping into simple humanism (Parker, 1999b). Reflexivity is often felt to be a kind of space that we can escape into as if we could then look upon the discipline from a distance, or reflexivity is sometimes even thought to be a solvent in which the abusive aspects of psychology can be dissolved. The activity of thinking back and thinking around an issue, and situating oneself, which is a valuable and necessary part of therapeutic work, is thought to illuminate all problems *and*, in that very process, solve them.

This is caricaturing a bit of course, but it is important to draw attention to the mistake sometimes made by radicals in the discipline when they imagine that to simply turn around and reflect on what we are doing, as researchers or practitioners, is enough. This is not to impugn critical reflection on our practices, and I want to draw a contrast between reflexivity as such and a *critical reflection*. While reflexivity is something that proceeds from within the interior of the self, and participates in all of the agonizing confessional work that Foucault (1976/1981) so brilliantly describes, critical reflection traces the subjective investments we make in our everyday practice, and traces them to the networks of institutional power that contain us.

While reflexivity can be a passive contemplative enterprise that all too often succeeds in paralysing the individual as they take responsibility for the pain and troubles of a painful and troubling set of circumstances, critical reflection is an active rebellious practice that drives the individual into action as they identify the exercise of power that pins them into place and the fault lines for the production of spaces of resistance. Although 'reflexivity' is often advertised by postmodernist writers as if that would serve as a solution to conceptual and social problems, at the very same time there is a sliding from term to term which sabotages the possibility of a critical vantage point being constructed from which to reflect critically on what is happening around the writer and why (Parker, 1992a).

Postmodernism and therapy

Family therapists and social workers who have been working through different systemic traditions are now arriving at an approach to presenting 'problems' as being located in discourses and narratives which structure families as well as identified patients within them, and quite of a few of these have been persuaded that they are 'postmodern' (McNamee and Gergen, 1992). The 'story metaphor' is seen as central to 'the philosophy of postmodernism' that brings these approaches together (McKenzie and Monk, 1997: 85). In some cases there is a hope that postmodernism will lead to a state of 'co-construction' in which 'psychotherapy practice as manipulation disappears' (Fruggeri, 1992: 45), or that this will mean that the clients are given 'a free conversational space' (Anderson and Goolishian, 1992: 29). Postmodernism here is being treated as if it were equivalent to Rortyesque liberal pragmatism in which all the problems disappear when we have conceptually 'deconstructed' them, and there is a debate now within this field of deconstructive therapy over the role of real problems and relatively enduring patterns of power (e.g. Parker, 1999c).

Postmodern sectors of capitalist culture

We can view the appearance and transformations of elements of modern *and* postmodern culture within the broader frame of contemporary capitalist culture – a culture underpinned for good and ill by the philosophers of the Western enlightenment – and in this way we can understand the way in which issues of autonomy and collectivism, scientism and fundamentalism operate through 'dialectical reversals' (Parker, 1998a). This theoretical stance avoids falling back into modern psychology in fright as an alternative to postmodern psychology. There is some understandable unease, for example, among narrative therapists who have enthusiastically taken a 'postmodern' turn because it seemed to invite a more ethical relationship to clients, that it may actually lead to something more akin to fundamentalism. Now we see concerns from those who have been advocating the postmodern turn in narrative therapy that this kind of 'narrative fundamentalism' (Amundson, 1994) will carry with it worrying moral political assumptions:

> Though the postmodern emphasis on stories or narratives (as opposed to theory or truth) is intended as a statement of modesty, there can be an easy slippage into the reification of Narrative as a foundational form of knowledge. This can in turn lead to implicit assumptions about 'better' and more 'appropriate' narratives for clients and to a notion of therapy as a form of story assessment and repair. In such a case, the appeal of postmodern plurality has been diverted into modern singularity.
> (Lowe, 1999: 82)

With respect to narrative therapies which now often characterize themselves as 'postmodern', it has been pointed out that these approaches which seem so thoroughly social still routinely appeal to the individual 'self' as a source of meaning and as the place to which all the reflexive capacities to engage in discursive activity will be traced (Newman and Holzman, 1996). For Kendall and Michael (1997: 12) this relationship is turned on its head with 'a dialectical view of psychology and the objects of psychological knowledge' blamed for the way postmodern (social) psychology slides into the idea that it might be possible to release individuality. Gergen, their object of scorn here, may indeed be guilty of appealing to some notion of the free individual who makes choices in the postmodern land of opportunity, but his celebration of autonomy in the midst of relationality needs to be understood as a part of a dialectical process *within* capitalist culture rather than a deliberate leitmotif of postmodern thought. Lowe's (1999) comment about 'postmodern multiplicity' threatening to give way to 'modern singularity' is pertinent. The issue here is that the 'modern singularity' being referred to is an organic motif of purification that has always carried with it particular dangers in capitalist culture.

What counts as 'self' is always defined in relation to an other, while othering proceeds through the constitution and unmaking of self. Therapeutic reflection can help us to follow this through, but it needs to break from modern psychology and postmodern psychology in order to do this adequately. 'What if there were no truth and no self?' a postmodernist might ask, and they may ask that because they want to deconstruct and disperse truth and self. What we must ask *before* we make that voluntarist leap to ridding ourselves of those relationships is *how* those relationships are sustained. It really does matter *how* we dissolve those relationships, *why* we do it and *when* we move into a serious reflection on what we are doing.

Conclusion

Cultural phenomena are not static, but they are characterized by certain distinctive features which mark them as coming from particular economic and political settings and as having emerged within certain intellectual and institutional contexts. By intellectual contexts here I mean the contradictory sites of reflection and resistance where organic intellectuals of many kinds crystallize and mobilize communities, and not only academic communities (Gramsci, 1971), and by institutional contexts I mean the various organizational settings where knowledge is formalized and sedimented and where people are encouraged and inhibited from thinking by practical-discursive formal communities, including academic ones (Kendall and Michael, 1997). One of my concerns about postmodernism in psychology is how we can maintain a dialectical tension between structure and topic and between seriousness and triviality. Which brings us back to the trivial example we opened the chapter with.

As well as the four possible theories about the story of Liam and Patsy's lost wedding, *The Guardian* floated another late alternative contender, that they had really got married after all. Sometimes it seems like it is too late, and we must either be with the radical postmoderns or with bad old reactionary psychology. This is not to say that advocates of postmodernism in psychology are unaware of the dilemma. In a presentation which challenged the form and content of traditional academic work, Mary Gergen explored some of the tensions between feminism and postmodernism, asking whether the relationship between the two would really work, whether it would be, as she put it, 'deadlock or wedlock' (Gergen and Gergen, 1995). Liam and Patsy did eventually get married, and they then separated after acrimonious public disputes.

We have to understand what the parameters of the choice might be, and to be careful now not simply to jump from the postmodern back to the modern. The problem is not so much that postmodern psychologists have jumped too far out of psychology but that they are still held in thrall by the still very powerful very modern discipline. The old paradigms are still in place, the cultural and economic societal conditions that made psychology possible still reign, realism is still used by psychology when it suits it and disregarded when it offers an account which conflicts with it, and psychology increasingly seduces people into psychology through therapeutic discourse. Now critical psychologists have the double task of combatting postmodern psychology's inability to move beyond the parameters of the discipline (either as its loyal friend or bewitched helpless mirror image) and combatting, as ever, old modern psychology.

3 Discourse analysis and psycho-analysis

This chapter, as the title indicates, connects discourse analysis with psychoanalysis. In the title I make a connection between the two approaches by hyphenating 'psycho-analysis'. In the early years of the approach that hyphen was usually used by psychoanalysts, and it is still sometimes favoured by those who use that hyphenated term to distinguish themselves from the followers of Jacques Lacan who adopt the more contemporary term 'psychoanalysis'. I draw attention to it here, because you will see that I do favour Lacanian readings of Freud as a way out of the biologically wired versions of development compatible with mainstream psychology.

The chapter treats psychoanalysis as a conceptual resource that should also be treated as a form of discourse. It thus enables an approach to research that does not reduce analysis to the level of the individual. I start with the point that discourse analysis presents a challenge to mainstream psychology but risks either neglecting individual experience by employing a quasi-behaviourist notion of 'blank subjectivity' or folding back into simple humanism through an appeal to 'uncomplicated subjectivity'.

Productive links can be made with psychoanalysis to elaborate an alternative notion of 'complex subjectivity' which would provide a better theory of the subject, and so circumvent these problems. Eight aspects of transformative theoretical work that would need to be applied to psychoanalytic writing – a move to a human science frame, a turn to collective phenomena, a shift away from always intentional authorial responsibility, a reading of

> texts as reconstructions of the past, an attention to researcher subjectivity, an understanding of the text as 'other', an emphasis on language in reframing accounts, and a sensitivity to the cultural specificity of analytic vocabularies – are described. Reflections on method, including a description of the 'discursive complex' as an analytic device, are outlined.

This chapter explores connections that might usefully be made between discourse analysis and psychoanalysis. These connections would respect both the social constructionist impulse of the discursive approach and the experiential insights of analytic work. Psychoanalysis would enable an account of the 'self' or 'subject' of discourse to be developed that both valued experience without essentializing it (the worry of those writers who resort to varieties of 'blank subjectivity') and located human experience without reducing it to an effect of language (the concern of those who indulge in a return to 'uncomplicated subjectivity').

It is not being proposed here that psychoanalysis should be looked to as a privileged and necessarily progressive alternative to behaviourist, cognitive or humanist psychology. Psychoanalysis itself has a dubious history and it often functions as a fixed interpretative system in the human sciences and an oppressive regime of truth in therapeutic practice. It will also be necessary, then, to *locate* psychoanalytic theory, and to view it as an account of subjectivity that is, like the rest of psychology, a culturally and historically specific system of 'self-reference', one of many ways for people to refer to and understand themselves. Indeed, it is precisely because it is powerful in Western culture that it should be taken seriously by social psychologists. It will be argued that the relationship between psychology as a closed theoretical apparatus of observation and regulation of behaviour and psychoanalysis as a more open conceptual system of speculative insights about the reproduction and transformation of experience constitutes psychoanalytic knowledge, at present, as a valuable source of theoretical and methodological ideas. This conceptual system can be opened up further and reworked to enrich discourse analysis.

The following sections of the chapter review the way that the figures of 'blank subjectivity' and 'uncomplicated subjectivity' are employed in contemporary discourse-analytic writing before turning to psychoanalytic theory as a resource for a more satisfactory account of the 'subject' in language. Eight transformations of psychoanalytic theory will then be described which would be necessary to bring this tradition of work into fruitful alliance with discourse analysis. The third section elaborates the figure of 'complex subjectivity' and a corresponding methodological device, the 'discursive complex'.

Discourse analysis

Discourse analysis sees language as something other than a simple transparent medium which enables the communication of thoughts from one person's head to another (Potter and Wetherell, 1987; Burman and Parker, 1993). Language provides the setting for thought and emotion such that we then think of, and feel, these phenomena to be things that always already existed fully formed inside ourselves. Different strands of language organize these things in competing, contradictory ways. Discourse analysis emphasizes variability in language rather than trying to discover some underlying consistent belief; it uncovers the functions language serves in different settings rather than seeing it as expressing something unconscious 'underneath'; and it is concerned with the way texts are constructed out of available symbolic resources rather than being made each time anew. People cannot invent the words and phrases appropriate to each occasion, or specific sets of feelings about things as they go along, but rather they must use already existing bits of language and sets of statements about the world, behaviour and internal mental states. These sets of statements are 'discourses', and in the process of using discourses, people find themselves caught up in meanings, connotations and feelings they cannot control. As well as moving language, then, people are moved by language. Discourse analysis is an example of the spread through various human sciences of the study of 'ordinary language' which was initiated by such writers as Austin (1962) and Wittgenstein (1958), and which has been linked to ethnomethodology and conversation analysis (e.g. Edwards and Potter, 1992). It has also been given a particular impetus and critical twist by the arrival of structuralist and post-structuralist ideas from France (e.g. Parker, 1992a).

The development of discursive psychology, and discursive work in social constructionist frameworks generally (Burr, 2003) provokes some important questions about the nature of the self or 'subject' as discourse-user. It is possible to identify two trends of work that have tried to tackle this issue. One trend (termed here 'blank subjectivity') deliberately ignores what is going on inside the person or what the history of their particular relationship to language may be, while the other trend (termed here 'uncomplicated subjectivity') returns to a humanist vision of the self as if it were autonomous and encountered language as a free agent.

Blank subjectivity

One reaction to traditional images of the individual in discursive psychology, and one that owes something to structuralist arguments as well as conversation-analytic and ethnomethodological empiricism (cf. Harré, 1981), has entailed a dismissal of individual experience as if it were only an effect of language or a work of fiction. The experience of the individual, in this view, could be seen as written through by discourses, and structuralist variants of the approach (e.g. Parker, 1992a) may sometimes seem to fall prey to this. The self may, in other ethnomethodologically inclined versions of discourse analysis, be described as if it were only an 'occasioned' rhetorical resource (e.g. Edwards and Potter, 1992). There is, in some writing, a sustained refusal of appeals to individual mental mechanisms or intentions beyond or outside what we can actually read in a text, and even questions about the 'stake' or 'interest' a speaking subject may have in a conversation is often reduced to the linguistic processes by which another speaker attributes such things (Edwards and Potter, 1992). Some worries about the determinism implied by this position have been expressed (e.g. Billig, 1991; Curt, 1994).

There is an understandable suspicion of psychological explanations in discourse analysis, though there are occasional sympathetic comments in the early literature about the value of cognitive psychology as a supplement to the study of language (Potter and Wetherell, 1987). Other writers working alongside the discursive tradition have followed a similar argument, though with a more explicit cognitivist ambition, and looked to other collective resources, such as 'social representations' to explain how individuals' minds work. Sometimes these resources are conceived of as formal structures that also exist inside people's heads, in the form of individual representations (Farr and Moscovici, 1984) or cognitive templates (Harré, 1979). These mechanisms then stand in for the subject, displacing it from centre-stage, rather than account for how experiences of agency are embedded in language and social practices. In some cases anti-Cartesian rhetoric is the warrant for an appeal to neuropsychology to close the gap once and for all between behaviour and the body in such a way as to blot out subjectivity (Harré and Gillett, 1994). There is a tendency in different varieties of discursive psychology, then, to treat the subject itself as a blank space.

Insofar as the position marked here as 'blank subjectivity' takes cultural forms seriously it deserves serious consideration. An attention to the production of memory and motivation in talk and to representations of self and identity have provided critical psychologists with powerful methodological resources for the detailed investigation and deconstruction of phenomena mainstream psychology takes for granted (Parker, 1996). However, it should be pointed out that an obstinate rejection of *any* attention to internal states, and the treatment of individual experience as no more than a stake in a blank space, can collapse pretty quickly into a simple humanist view of the person when it is put under pressure. All of the writers cited here do want to avoid the accusation that their description of speech is simple behaviourism or empiricism, and they recognize that a strict and thorough view of the subject as a blank space around which discourse circulates is untenable.

The problem is that an acknowledgement of the limitations of a 'blank subjectivity' position is not enough to solve the problem that it sets up, for an attempt to balance a refusal to theorize subjectivity with an attempt to take agency on board leads, instead, to another problem. For what is deliberately avoided or unexamined at one moment, the human agent, will then be seen as entirely unproblematic the next. The very refusal to explore the nature of subjectivity will lead to it creeping in again untheorized and unreconstructed, whether this as universal dilemmatic reasoning qualities of human cognition (e.g. Billig, 1991) or descriptions of how a discourse-user may intend their rhetoric to function in a conversation (e.g. Edwards, 1995). This has provided a curious point of connection with a second strand of work in recent psychology which is more sympathetic to humanism but which operates as a simple mirror image of the account offered by advocates of the 'blank subjectivity' position.

Uncomplicated subjectivity

The attempt to escape the limitations of 'blank subjectivity' has led to a celebration of a second rhetorical figure that can be termed 'uncomplicated subjectivity'. Here, a genuine worry about the absence of the 'self' in discursive psychology has prompted appeals to some variety of 'core self' which is able to choose which discourses or interpretative repertoires to use in different situations (e.g. Burr, 2003). This is uncomfortably close to the traditional humanist fantasy of the pure subject as an active reflective independent agent. It presupposes a self who uses discourse rather than looking at how specific theories of the self develop and then become living spaces for subjects to inhabit.

There is also, as a corollary of this, a revival in some forms of qualitative research in psychology, of the assumption that what we will find and know could be a kind of 'mirror of nature' (Rorty, 1980), and here the nature of the subject who is the reflexive agent is assumed to be pre-given. It is as if the self is there before, and independent of social context. Qualitative alternatives social psychology which draw upon sociology, particularly from the 'grounded theory' tradition (Glaser and Strauss, 1967; Henwood and Pidgeon, 1992), is founded on this notion of the subject. It is argued in that literature that the discovery and 'saturation' of categories in research material through exhaustive coding is simply a function of the researcher looking very carefully as if they were able to abandon all preconceptions. The researcher as subject here is seen as the mirror for the meanings in the text, and it is often assumed that those meanings are the same meanings that have been created and left in the text by other subjects. Despite its forceful critique of objectification in quantitative approaches, this alternative tradition of qualitative research promotes an intuitivist form of empiricism in which the subjectivity of the researcher is sovereign.

This raises a host of problems for social psychologists wanting to strike a distance from essentialist and individualist arguments. The notion of 'uncomplicated subjectivity' is one that has been challenged in critical work inspired by post-structuralism, where it has been described as a version of the rational 'unitary subject' of the Cartesian tradition (Henriques *et al.*, 1998; Hollway, 1989). This critical work has drawn heavily upon psychoanalytic ideas to question the way psychology reduces social phenomena to fixed qualities of individual minds. We need to consider carefully what psychoanalysis has to offer, though, before elaborating a third, more adequate, mode of subjectivity. Rather than simply assuming that psychoanalysis will help us, we have to understand how it functions as a kind of knowledge about the self, and why it may then be useful for opening up texts.

Psycho-analysis

Psychoanalysis haunts psychology. It is the discipline's 'repressed other' (Burman, 1994), an account of subjectivity that the discipline systematically excludes but requires to complement positivist neglect of human experience in most of its models of the person. The history of psychology is also the history of forgotten links with the psychoanalytic tradition. Three broken links from the 1920s, now erased from the memory of psychology in most textbooks, can be seen as symptomatic: the neuropsychologist A.R. Luria took a leading role in the founding of the Russian Psychoanalytic Society (Roudinesco, 1990); the cognitive-developmental writer Jean Piaget was a member of the International Psychoanalytical Association (IPA) and undertook a personal analysis with the Jungian Sabina Spielrein (Roudinesco, 1990); and the experimental psychologist E.G. Boring went into analysis to work through his feelings about transference to Titchener that emerged during the writing of his *History of Experimental Psychology* (Parker, 1989).

It might be tempting, in the light of these surprising historical connections, to simply turn back to psychoanalytic theory as if it were a full-blown progressive alternative to academic psychology with a ready-made theory of the subject for discursive psychology which would transform our research, but we should be aware that it is not beyond the wits of the discipline to accommodate some psychoanalytic ideas and remain exactly as it is. North American developmental psychology is happy to embrace the work of Daniel Stern (1985), for example, partly because Stern reproduces and reinforces an image of the self suffused with North American ideology (Cushman, 1991). Mainstream psychology has long been afflicted by a sterile opposition between positivist avoidance of experience and humanist celebrations of it. Psychoanalysis can all too easily, then, be recruited into this institutionally sanctioned dualism.

It is also important to be aware, then, of another history of repression, that which operates over the border in the field of psychoanalysis itself. There is a politically radical tradition in psychoanalysis, from Otto Fenichel and Wilhelm Reich (Jacoby, 1983) to Marie Langer (1989) and to Slavoj Žižek (1989), which is obscured in the official publications of the International Psychoanalytical Association. There is also a theoretically radical (though often politically dubious) Lacanian school which has at present (though one would not guess it from IPA literature) the allegiance of half the practising analysts in the world. There is a risk even here, though, to radical work in and against traditional psychology, for even these most progressive strands of psychoanalytic theory present themselves as if they were dealing in 'Truth' and so support the status quo (Prilleltensky, 1994).

It may sometimes be appropriate to employ psychoanalytic theory to understand social phenomena as if that theory were the best framework, and there is strong tradition of research now available to psychologists ranging from those using Frankfurt school writings (Elliott, 1992) to Lacanian work (Hollway, 1989) and British object relations theory (Frosh, 1991). The claim being made here is more sceptical about psychoanalytic truth claims, however. Rather than treat psychoanalysis simply as a key to unlock the secrets of the subject, we should reflect upon how it has been fashioned as part of a particular system of self-talk and self-reference in Western culture. Psychoanalytic theory is treated here as a powerful framework because psychoanalytic knowledge helps structure the dominant culture in the West.

It would be possible to elaborate alternative accounts of the subject in social psychology which would link discourse analysis with, for example, a self-categorization perspective (Reicher, 1996). While such a 'cognitive' subject is also present in Western culture (and the reason why such a theoretical framework makes sense to us in the first place), the argument in this chapter is that we need to take seriously one of the most powerful forms of subjectivity that circulate around us and within us. Subjectivity which is elaborated in the discourse of Western culture also takes on a psychoanalytic character, whether we like it or not. We need to play a double-game with psychoanalysis in social psychology by taking a further critical step, then, to embed psychoanalytic vocabulary in culture, as a culturally and locally bounded discourse, and to treat the psychoanalytic institution as a 'regime of truth' with effects of power no less reactionary than those of psychology itself (Foucault, 1976/1981; Masson, 1992).

Psychoanalysis and discursive approaches

The development of discursive approaches in psychology has encouraged a critical reflection upon the truth effects of all forms of psychological talk. For that reason discourse analysis provides a useful point of purchase from which to view psychoanalysis, and a theoretical framework that could potentially wield it to good effect.

Discourse analysis, in common with the rest of psychology, normally tries not to get embroiled in psychoanalytic theory. This is because psychoanalysis too often, in common with the rest of psychology, tries to discover what is going on inside the individual who speaks or writes, as if that would adequately explain underlying motives and causes for behaviour. The suspicion of psychoanalytic reductionism among discourse analysts is understandable, but discourse analysis surely does need some account of how it is that a speaker and writer, or a listener and reader, is moved by language. Some of the reinterpretations of Freud that have been washed up with post-structuralism are helpful, and some forms of discourse analysis have attempted to use psychoanalysis in this way (Hollway, 1989; Parker, 1992a). Lacan's (2006) work has been particularly influential here, for aspects of his reading of Freud which emphasize processes occurring within language inspired the revival of psychoanalysis in cultural studies, and more recently in social psychology. The practice of psychoanalysis is a 'talking cure' which is rooted in theories of language (Forrester, 1980). We need, however, to *locate* psychoanalytic theory in language if it is to be a helpful addition to a critical social constructionist vision of discursive psychology as culturally specific, mutable and self-transformative.

A reading of culture as a meshwork of discourses which can be analytically decomposed needs to be connected here with a cultural history of the different forms of subjectivity, including psychoanalytic subjectivity, that are constituted for readers now. Psychoanalytic notions which thread through Western twentieth-century culture simultaneously carry discourses and elaborate sets of subject positions for actors in texts and for readers of texts. Discursive forms in contemporary Western culture are patterns of meaning that systematically form objects and subjects, and their internal structure often derives from psychoanalytic discourse. Notions of childhood 'complex', the 'ego' and the 'unconscious' together with the panoply of strategies that one may use to reflect upon these objects ('acting out', 'repetition', 'working through', etc.) circulate as elements of self-understanding in Western culture. A psychoanalytically informed discourse reading would not treat these notions as pre-given, but would look to the ways in which *texts* reproduce such categories, and reproduce subjects who can make sense of the texts that hold them. This point will be returned to below. First, eight points of transformation which will help us to connect psychoanalysis with discourse-analytic perspectives will be identified. These eight points will also help us to elaborate an alternative to 'blank' and 'uncomplicated' accounts of subjectivity.

Psychoanalysis into discourse

These eight transformations of psychoanalytic discourse open up the Freudian and post-Freudian theoretical apparatus as a resource for discourse analysts. The transformations displayed here are not intended to warrant psychoanalysis as a 'correct' theory of subjectivity which would then be applicable to every culture. It is because psychoanalytic discourse saturates culture that we need to use that theoretical framework to unravel the texts we live in (Parker, 1997).

Human science

The first point of transformation is the shifting of psychoanalysis from the realm of the natural sciences to that of the human sciences. There are already precedents for this move inside psychoanalytic discourse. Bettelheim (1986) argues that Freud was working in the context of a culture in which there was an acknowledged distinction between the *Naturwissenschaften*, the natural sciences such as biology, chemistry and physics on the one hand, and the *Geisteswissenschaften*, the sciences of the spirit, human sciences such as psychology, philosophy and literature on the other. It does seem, as Grünbaum (1984) has pointed out, that Freud himself was much of the time appealing to the natural sciences, but we can still read Bettelheim's humanist reworking of psychoanalysis as an injunction to question standard positivist criteria of experimentation, hypothesis testing and falsification. We should then, instead, employ criteria which respect interpretation, experiential resonance and understanding in our readings of texts.

Habermas (1972) makes a similar point, and goes a bit further when he argues that psychoanalysis should not be seen as either a natural science or human science but as an *emancipatory* science. Cultural analysis as 'applied psychoanalysis' would then be committed to a reflective and progressive moral position (Wolfenstein, 1991). It would also then be possible to tie it to a deliberative moral/political standpoint in which the oppressive practices of the institution of psychology, and psychoanalysis too for that matter, can be unmasked (e.g. Parker, 1994). Both Bettelheim and Habermas value the reflexive capacities of human beings to challenge and transform self-limiting relationships and societal structures. Psychoanalysis, like psychology, often threatens to only look in at the self rather than out at the limits, and so we need to locate our understanding of reflexivity in the collective character of human psychology.

Collective phenomena

The second point, which connects us with long-standing debates in and against the psychoanalytic movement, is that psychoanalysis should look to the collective cultural resources that structure our sense of ourselves and those aspects of our lives that lie outside conscious awareness. The turn away from a scientific and materialist account of the mind and to the realms of art and mythology as an alternative foundation for psychoanalysis free of any pretence to be any kind of science goes back, of course, to Jung (1983). Freud's attempts to delve into anthropology and to propose Lamarckian models of the acquisition of historical memories was driven, in part, by his dislike of Jungian mysticism (Gay, 1988). It is possible to take up the Jungian argument that there is some form of 'collective unconscious' but to see this as a historically constituted symbolic resource rather than something lying in a mysterious spiritual realm. Collective resources would then be seen not as floating beneath the personal unconscious of each of us, but as *within* an 'unconscious' textual realm, the realm of discourse. A multiplicity of tacit understandings, unacknowledged assumptions and unintended consequences frame our lives as we encounter and manage texts and social practices. Discourse analysis helps us to explore how those texts and practices are put together, but we also need to go beyond that to look at how we reproduce and transform those texts and practices in ways which may be either self-defeating or empowering (Parker, 1992a).

There are some similarities between this position and that advocated by Vološinov (1973), which, although critical of Freudian discourse, elaborated many psychoanalytic tenets into a linguistically based system. Collective textual phenomena would then be closer to a transpersonal level of meaning that Foulkes (1964), writing in the group analysis tradition, refers to, or to the unconscious as an aspect of the Symbolic order that Lacan (2006) describes. The unconscious is then itself treated, as Lacan argued it should be, as 'the discourse of the Other' (with the 'Other' here being the symbolic system that holds culture in place and determines the location of each individual speaking subject). This notion of the unconscious also extends one of the most important discourse-analytic principles, that of insistent variation, inconsistency of sense in language. It allows us to develop an account of tacit assumptions, unacknowledged conditions and unintended consequences *and* account for the contradictory ways in which these mesh with structures of power that are relayed through texts.

Psychoanalysis as a form of reading

This brings us to the third point which is to do with issues of authorship and responsibility. Psychoanalysis does usually try to trace the meanings it interprets to the desires or motives of an individual. Even if the more humanist analysts want to tell the patient that the latent meanings are there 'as well as' what appears on the surface rather than 'instead of' (Hobson, 1985), there is still too often a concern with encouraging the patient to take responsibility for what they have done or said (Lomas, 1977). There has been a shift away from this position following developments in literary theory, with the argument that we should celebrate, in Barthes' (1967) phrase, the 'death of the author', the end of attempts to trace all meaning to the individual producer, and look to dynamic processes that operate independently of the author, or of the speaker.

This move is also important if a psychoanalytic discursive psychology is to escape the charge that it is necessarily reductionist (Billig, 1976). In cultural analysis it would not be helpful always to try to identify the 'author' of statements about the phenomenon we are concerned with. The writers that are quoted in a piece of analysis may be pathological in some way, but speculation at this level would be reductionist and, in psychoanalytic terms, a 'wild analysis'. A symptomatic reading of texts as ideological forms should be tied to a view of them as implicated in systems of power that are not reducible to the intentions of any particular individual. Subjects are then positioned in these texts, and the contradictory patterns of the text together with the contradictory patterns of life narrative that carry the subject through the text provide spaces for certain kinds of emotional investment.

Memory and history as textuality

The fourth point of transformation, moving further away from the author, prompts us to take as our object of study the *text* and to reflect upon the way that we gather together, as part of the single research text we analyse, a number of different bits of text. The phenomena we are focusing upon may be explored through studying interviews, discussion groups, newspaper articles, advertisements, books or novels or graffiti, television programmes or computer games. These different bits of text, and the commentary on them, and the discussion of that commentary can be treated as one mass of material, one research text. This view of textuality has important implications for notions of memory and history, for versions of reality are now seen as 'storied' into being with their social construction bound up with power (Stenner and Eccleston, 1994). The turn to the text as a site for mental processes has already been anticipated in psychoanalysis.

Individual memory, in Lacanian psychoanalysis, is seen as a process of 'deferred action' in which there is always a reconstruction of the past in the present, but a reconstruction that takes place around real events (and this is something which differentiates the Lacanian account from Jungian views of the past as indifferent to the real). This bears some similarities with the view that collective memory, in discourse, is present in the text, the text we read now in the present (Middleton and Edwards, 1990). When we read a text analytically, following Saussure (1974), we are able to view it, as a system of 'differences' which produces a sense of what there was 'before' it. This system of differences and oppositions is realized in everyday talk and thought as a system of dilemmas in discourse, in which each proposition poses an explicit or implicit contrary position (cf. Billig, 1987). The play of differences as polarities marked by contradiction, by ambivalence also connects discourse dynamics with psychodynamics (Parker, 1992a), and may allow us then to avoid discursive relativism (e.g. Edwards *et al.*, 1995) in favour of an account of history that asks what has been repressed from the account, and *why* that may be (e.g. Gill, 1995). The point here is not that psychoanalysis offers us a 'correct' or 'true' standpoint from which to assess which accounts are closer to reality than others. Rather, an attention to the way accounts *exclude* different perspectives as a function of a historical process of cultural production and power allows us to locate relativism itself as a particular kind of reading strategy. This textual transformation of psychoanalysis locates micro-processes of memory construction in the context of wider symbolic systems of cultural memory, and it is able to explore the ways in which symbolic systems are interwoven with, constitute and are constituted by real historical events.

Researcher subjectivity

The last point, which raised questions about what is at stake for different readers in historical analysis and reconstruction, brings us to the next, fifth transformation which brings us face to face with the emotional investment we have in research material as listeners or readers. Our analysis is informed by our place in the text. The position of the researcher plays a part in the interpretation of a piece of text, and a reflection on this relationship between the researcher and the text departs from traditional positivist approaches, in which there is a sustained pretence that this relationship can be avoided.

There are issues here of 'counter-transference', meant in the broadest sense of the term as researcher interest and involvement (Hunt, 1989). How does the text move us, and what have we brought to it of ourselves? Some free association around the material is a useful part of the analysis, and a variety of techniques from psychoanalysis may be helpful. We can consider the text as a dream, for example, and work through layers of secondary revision (distortions of meaning to fit present-day settings), and analyse condensation (in the functioning of metaphors in the text) and displacement from significant aspects of the material (in instances of metonymy), and produce representations that try to capture some of the images that underlie the surface narratives. But we need here to be aware of *ourselves* as the dreamers, for in the case of popular fictions or beliefs, unlike instances of other people telling us their dreams, we understand and share, partially at least, at some level, the story. As Barthes (1967) puts it, with the death of the author comes the birth of the reader.

The form of discourse analysis that emerges in this activity of close reading is part of a burgeoning school of qualitative research in psychology which deconstructs the opposition between objectivity and subjectivity. Subjectivity is not treated, as it is conventionally in psychology, as the idiosyncratic perspective of an individual disconnected from the shared 'objective' reality of the scientific community. Rather, the 'objective' position is seen as thoroughly subjective itself, for it is an attempt to keep a distance from the topic. Subjectivity in research can then be employed as a resource for the reading, a resource that then drives us to as close as we could be to an 'objective' account (Parker, 1994). This also, incidentally, connects the reading more closely with the Lacanian tradition in which the analyst does not 'know', is not the 'expert', than to the North American and IPA model of the analyst as operating through forms of ego which have a more veridical perception of reality. This is also, then, the basis for a better model of research in psychology.

The text as 'other'

The sixth point of conceptual transformation concerns the way we respond to the text not only as something we participate in, but also as material that is 'other' to us. It will be suggested here that we should treat the overall text as if it were a 'subject'. This move, of course, risks drawing us back into problems of reductionism, with a macro-reduction to a sociological level taking the place of orthodox psychological micro-reductionism to the individual or, in the case of conversation analysis, to specific turns in a conversation. To treat the text as a subject opens the text up to be read as a system of defence mechanisms and as a system of symptoms. On the one hand this follows and extends the development of psychoanalysis as a form of hermeneutics discussed by Habermas (1972) for example, in which institutions can be decoded through an analysis of the distortions, seen as defence mechanisms, in the discourse they employ. On the other hand it follows the use of psychoanalysis as ideology-critique by Žižek (1989) which treats symptoms as breakdowns in communication which express and so reveal the very system of distortions they attempt to mask.

Defences and symptoms, then, are seen here as part of the structure of the text, and analysis helps us understand that *structure* itself rather than opening up what is hidden 'underneath'. A reading of text which locates rhetorical strategies in systems of power, and asks how certain visions of the world and positions for subjects are privileged and how other accounts are obscured is already, of course, a 'symptomatic' reading. The text can be treated as a system of defences and discursive operations which guarantee its place in a regime of truth. The text is treated as if it were a person, the second analytic move, in the same kind of way that a person is treated as a text in psychoanalysis, the first analytic move, but in such a way as to retain the first analytic move, and to embed the subject as text in the text as subject. The person is treated as if they were a text, as if their life narrative and position in discourse comprised a network of symbolic material that could be read for different kinds of significance in relation to different kinds of institution and cultural phenomena. A cultural text is treated in the same kind of way, as inhabiting certain networks of relationships with other texts, and both text and individual are treated as embedded in other texts. Taken in this way, this move reverses, but does not annul the traditional psychoanalytic concern to treat the person as a text; it both, in dialectical terms, challenges and completes that concern. It is not being suggested, then, that the text is a person with, for example, a childhood history, but that a text *may* in some cases be structured around Oedipal structures which position particular individuals who move within it and elaborate it as they speak.

Psychoanalysis as a language

The revisions of Freud advertised in this chapter that render him helpful as a guide in the reading of all sorts of texts rest on an important assumption, a seventh point concerning terminology. Alongside Bettelheim's (1986) argument that Freud was working in the human sciences, and as evidence for that claim, retranslations have been offered of the rather mechanistic and impersonal terms in the *Standard Edition* (Freud, 1953–1974) such as 'ego', 'instincts', 'cathexis' and the 'mental apparatus' as, respectively, the 'I', the 'drives', 'investment' and the 'soul'. It is claimed that the standard mis-translations transform the poetic and allusive writings of Freud into statements of 'fact' (Timms and Segal, 1988). If a psychoanalytic reading is to be plausible it must beware both of talking of 'facts' and of using jargon.

A particular danger is that we might resort to the simple translation of the language of the text into psychoanalytic language. The analysis or, in this case, discourse analysis must make sense in a language that connects with the experience of the reader. At the same time an analysis also has to go beyond the text to a deeper understanding (Wolfenstein, 1991). The use of a particular psychoanalytic system should, if it is to be worthwhile, carry with it something more than a simple re-phrasing of the text in its own terms; it should produce with that re-phrasing a yield of understanding in which we are positioned in relation to the text in a different way. Here, theoretical work will be necessary in order to locate the text in historical context and structures of power. This is something that should accompany all versions of discourse-analytic work whether they are psychoanalytic or not.

Cultural specificity

These different psychoanalytic resources with their competing vocabularies bring us to the final, eighth, point of transformation which is that there is not one correct interpretation, or one correct psychoanalytic system for the wording of an interpretation. It is possible that the cultural location of psychoanalytic systems (Lacan in France, Habermas in Germany, Žižek in Slovenia) makes them specifically applicable to their cultures. However, when translated across the geographical, linguistic and political boundaries that mark off sectors of Western culture, they then each hook something in us. It is in the nature of the unconscious (the unconscious produced for us in culture now) to be riven by contradictory meanings, to tolerate these contradictions, and to smooth them over. It is in the nature of psychoanalysis as a rational therapeutic enterprise or as a theoretical framework in the human sciences, here as discourse analysis, to notice contradiction. We struggle, then, over the tension between different contradictory understandings. It is partly because of this chaotic and complex unconscious network of meanings that pervade language that it is better to talk of 'understanding' here rather than to refer to 'explanation' in discursive research.

The use of different psychoanalytic vocabularies will be appropriate for different cultural phenomena. The prescriptions for subjectivity laid down by the US 'ego-psychologists', for example, may be relevant to describe institutions which predict and control human psychology, and those prescriptions may be seen as reproduced by mainstream psychological institutions (Parker, 1994). The particular preoccupations of the Lacanian school, to take another example, may be relevant to describe forms of experience in sectors of modern life where the self is fragmented and captured by symbolic systems (Parker, 1997). Each version of psychoanalysis has an appeal within specific cultural arenas, and it would be a mistake to propose one version as applicable to all. The writings of Deleuze and Guattari (1977), for example, present a 'schizoanalysis' which resists other varieties of psychoanalysis, particularly those which present the family form and the Oedipus complex as necessary to healthy mental development (see Chapter 4 of this book), but it would be little more than wish-fulfilment to pretend that most actual social situations display that resistance. We need to attend to the varieties of subjectivity that coexist in modern culture, and the fault lines for reflection and resistance will be distinct, and with more or less room for movement.

Subjectivity in discourse

To understand *why* psychoanalysis helps us in understanding ourselves and the discourses we use to reflect upon our social behaviour and inner mental processes, we need to look at the ways in which psychoanalysis has spread as a form of self-understanding through Western culture and at the ways in which it has become part of the theories of self that persons employ to make sense of themselves (Moscovici, 1976/2008; Parker, 1997). Here, we should consider first the forms of selfhood that have been produced for us as discursive environments that we inhabit, develop and challenge in everyday life in the twenty-first-century Western world. We will then be in a better position to analyse the discursive configurations which structure, facilitate and limit how we might make and remake ourselves in different social contexts.

Complex subjectivity

This brings us to a third approach which may circumvent some of the contradictions that attend the figures of 'blank subjectivity' and 'uncomplicated subjectivity' (and the ways in which they complement one another). One way forward is through developing an account of what can be termed 'complex subjectivity' in which a sense of agency is tangled up in cultural forms. This figure of subjectivity looks to the way in which the subject is always complicated by its enmeshment in particular dominant cultural forms pertaining to self-knowledge that circulate in the surrounding society. The figure of 'complex subjectivity' is one that takes seriously both the intentions and desires of the individual and the operation of social structures and discourse. A crucial part of this third notion of subjectivity, however, is that the cultural elements out of which a distinct sense of individuality are forged must be attended to. Here, the social constructionist positions advanced by Harré (1983, 1986b) and Shotter (1984, 1993) on the formation of the self and an inner emotional life through the internalization of shared representations of individuality are relevant. It is here that psychoanalysis starts to become important, for psychoanalysis operates as a form of self-knowledge in Western culture, and enters into subjectivity to complicate it all the further. Forms of culture are represented in texts, and so also in the subjectivity of those who can make sense of them as they read them, and we need to take seriously the way in which psychoanalytic culture is transmitted in discourse (directly or indirectly, deliberately or unintentionally).

One of the founding texts of the social representations tradition (Moscovici, 1976/2008), supports the argument being advanced here relating to the nature of shared psychological knowledge in contemporary culture. Moscovici (1976/2008) traced the suffusion of psychoanalysis through popular culture in France, and his detailed study of the social representation of psychoanalysis is paralleled by sociological work in America (Berger, 1965) and Britain (Bocock, 1976) which has traced the 'cultural affinity' of contemporary culture with psychoanalytic categories. This account is then compatible with a social constructionist view of the cultural transmission of psychological knowledge from the social through to the interior of the subject (Parker, 1997). At the present time, in much of this culture, complex subjectivity is also, to some extent, psychoanalytic subjectivity, and this then has repercussions for the methods that could be developed within a discursive framework.

Discourse analysis which takes these cultural forms seriously would need to attend to the ways in which language is structured, not only around 'interpretative repertoires' (Potter and Wetherell, 1987) or 'discourses' (Parker, 1992a), but also around 'discursive complexes'. 'Interpretative repertoires' are useful for highlighting the alternative ways in which a person in a conversation or an interview may frame an issue, and 'discourses' capture the way in which such different frames participate in wider cultural patterns of meaning. 'Discursive complexes' take this analysis a step further with a description of forms of subjectivity that circulate in a culture as a function of discourse and of the theories of self that subjects in a culture elaborate for themselves in relation to different phenomena.

Discursive complexes

The methodological device of the 'discursive complex' captures the twofold nature of psychoanalytic discourse. The term 'complex' is used quite deliberately here to evoke the peculiarly Freudian and post-Freudian nature of the subjectivity we live so much of the time. Were we to study behavioural or cognitive notions conveyed in language and experienced by users, we would perhaps want to speak of 'discursive repertoires' or 'discursive templates'. Self-categorization perspectives on the subject as discourse-user would also pick up on cognitive discourse to elaborate a version of subjectivity (Reicher, 1996). Discursive complexes pick up and reflect upon psychoanalytic discourse which circulates through culture. On the one hand the concepts that psychoanalytic texts employ are relayed through culture as components of a discourse, as objects that are circumscribed by definitions in academic and professional writing and in use in popular media, in everyday talk. In this sense, the discourse constitutes places for subjects to come to be, whether that is as the child with problems separating from the mother, the teenager filled with frustration and resentment at authority, or the older adult reflecting on an unfulfilled life and needs.

The discourse thus *positions* the subject who is addressed by or is employing the discourse to understand themselves or troubling relationships (cf. Davies and Harré, 1990; Hollway, 1989; Stenner, 1993). On the other hand, the discourse touches an already existing shape of subjectivity for those who write and speak about themselves and others, whether that is in the form of autobiography or advice column, in a television interview or on the couch with a therapist. It chimes with a theory of self that the subject has been invited to elaborate for themselves many times in this culture, and so it reconfigures each time some of the emotions that are available to them. As the discourse makes certain types of experience salient to the subject, it also provides an explanation for aspects of experience that have as yet slipped the web of discourse. There is thus a yield of self-understanding which simultaneously locks the subject into the systems of talk that comprise the communities in which they live. The discursive complex not only exists for the individual subject, then, but also provides the medium through which subjects may render themselves one to another as having like psychological properties, as women, for example, or men (Parker, 1995).

This analytic device can also attend, then, to the experiential dimension of language-use. A discursive complex is tuned to the complex subjectivity, the psychoanalytic subjectivity which is constituted for culturally competent members and provoked moment by moment in child-rearing practices, self-improvement manuals, therapeutic group settings of every kind, and in versions of psychoanalysis in popular culture (cf. Riley, 1983). The subject positions that are made available in Western culture are invested with attention and affect that then 'holds' the subject in a particular relation to others. Discursive complexes which operate according to psychoanalytic principles structure locations in the linguistic sphere, on the surface, and simultaneously inscribe psychodynamic forms of feeling on subjects as beings with a sense of 'depth' (Foucault, 1976/1981).

Every culture produces complications for the experience of subjectivity among its members, and it is difficult to imagine a human community that enjoys direct and immediate communication between people. Sometimes that complication and confusion is through religious and ideological mystification, overt coercion, threats and fear. It is also always through the operation of orders of discourse which determine what may and may not be said (Foucault, 1969/1972). Research on social representations has gone some way to successfully addressing this task of cultural analysis (Farr and Moscovici, 1984; Moscovici, 1976/2008), but the contribution of a combination of discourse-analytic research and psychoanalytic theory could also be of value here.

Conclusion

The analytic frame of reference that is being proposed in this chapter carries with it particular dangers that mirror those that attend traditional psychology. Psychoanalysis has a history of imperialist ambition as an endeavour that attempts to find hidden unconscious motives that underlie behaviour in all individuals in all cultures in all historical periods. Discourse analysis has been a valuable development for critics in psychology who have wanted to problematize the knowledge in this discipline, and it would be an irony indeed if advocates of discourse analysis let go of psychology only to fall into the arms of something worse. It has been argued in this chapter that psychoanalysis needs to be reworked to make it sensitive to social constructionist accounts of the subject, and that the role of psychoanalytic theory in the wider culture is such that this is a necessary task for a properly social constructionist psychology. If we are to take culture seriously in psychological research, we also need to take psychoanalysis seriously, and we can do so if it is treated as a discursive form which were then turned to good effect in critical transformative psycho-analytic discourse-analytic research.

4 Discursive complexes in material culture

In this chapter I take up the notion of 'discursive complexes' that I introduced in the last chapter. I tried to be clear when I introduced the notion that I did not mean it to be a way of smuggling in psychoanalytic explanation back into psychology. Psychoanalysis as theory of childhood and personality has often operated as a form of psychology just as normalizing (defining what is normal and making people conform to those definitions) and pathologizing (labelling people who do not fit within psychologically defined images of normality) as other approaches in the discipline.

Discourse analysis, of course, gives us an opportunity not only to focus on the organization of language itself rather than what is going on inside people's heads, but also on the way this language contains images of normality and pathology. This means that a discourse-analytic approach should also treat psychoanalytic explanation as a form of language. The discursive complex is therefore concerned with the way psychoanalytic forms of subjectivity are carried through language, and this chapter shows, through a worked empirical example, how it is possible to develop a reading of text that employs psychoanalytic theory – here from Gilles Deleuze and Félix Guattari – in a non-reductionist manner. This does not mean that Deleuze and Guattari are correct, just that their ideas are influential or that they neatly summarize some popular psychoanalytic ideas.

The position of the researcher as subject is a crucial element in a psychoanalytic reading of texts, and so the chapter opens with theoretical reflections upon the role of method in the version of

64 *Discursive complexes in material culture*

> discourse analysis presented here. The empirical part of the chapter is designed to illustrate how forms of psychoanalytic subjectivity circulate through culture and are then represented to the reader. The discussion explores implications of the approach for qualitative research in psychology.

The text from the back of a tube of children's toothpaste would appear, at first sight, to be a both innocent and trivial fragment of contemporary common sense. 'Common sense' is usually a good deal less innocuous than it pretends to be, however, and it replays taken-for-granted descriptions of, and prescriptions for, what it is to be an acceptable member of a culture. Of the many varieties of discourse analysis inside and outside psychology, the form influenced by post-structuralist debates has been most useful in unravelling the webs of ideology that inhere in popular culture (and in psychology). Discourse analysis here deconstructs, with the help of Foucault's (1975/1977, 1976/1981) observations on modern subjectivity, the intimate link between language and power in 'common sense' (Parker, 1992a). What seems trivial can be seen as symptomatic of patterns of regulation, and the toothpaste text in question can now no longer be read with an innocent eye. An examination of culture, that which is usually taken to be exterior to the subject as researcher, could be a simple elaboration of discourses as sets of statements which construct objects, but it is now also necessary to enter analytic space, that which is interior to the subjectivity of the researcher. This move, which is ostensibly reductive, apparently individualist, is actually a move deeper into culture itself.

A Foucauldian discourse-analytic reading of this toothpaste text (Banister *et al.*, 1994) makes a number of assumptions about the nature of language as well as the positions set up for subjects as actors in the text and as addressees of the 'messages'. These assumptions (and the messages) carry with them culturally prescribed understandings about the nature of subjectivity in the circumambient culture. In this chapter we can go further to explore the way in which the assumptions in turn entail some employment of psychoanalytic categories. Although Foucault (1976/1981) himself was concerned with psychoanalysis as a form of confession, psychoanalytic notions also underpin images of the body as compliant with, and resistant to, language in his work. Foucault (1969/1972) anticipates discussions of variation, function and construction in discourse analysis in social psychology (Potter and Wetherell, 1987), and points towards the elaboration of these aspects of language in psychoanalytic terms. Let us take these three assumptions about the nature of discourse in turn, and follow through that analytic dynamic.

A first assumption concerns variation. The assumption is that the host of connotations that dance on each pinpoint of the text are all relayed, at some level, to the reader. While all the varieties of meaning could simply be seen as conveyed to the reader at a 'non-conscious' level, in a realm of processing 'outside awareness', specific psychoanalytic notions of representation are required to account for how the meanings operate alongside and against one another. The multiple semiotics of the packet and written instructions are seen as 'overdetermined' (that is, arising from many different patterns of meaning at one and the same time). The space for one meaning does not prohibit another from functioning, and the meanings do not necessarily operate upon the reader sequentially. The text, like the unconscious, is seen as knowing no time nor logical contradiction, in the sense that variation, as illogical contradiction, reigns as a condition for what we take to be coherence (as we fix one meaning and disregard the others that are necessary to give it a particular context and form). It matters to us, of course, that the meanings in the text flood into the subject whether they know it or not or want that to happen, and any discourse-analytic reading of texts is to some extent therapeutic.

A second assumption concerns function, and the way that the text produces certain effects upon a reader. Once we break from seeing function as the deliberate exercise of 'interests', we move into the realm of the unconscious, and of unconscious meanings addressing and catching the reader's unconscious. The experience of the reader as addressee is transformed in the process of reading such that they are locked in some way into the discursive structure of the text. One way of conceptualizing this, following Althusser's (1971) account of the work of ideology, is to say that the reader is 'interpellated', or hailed by the text, and that any response to the text, whether that response indicates agreement with the message, or resistance to the claims the text is making about the nature of the reader and prescriptions for action being formulated for them, is conditioned by this interpellation. A good way of describing this process is to employ the notion of 'subject position', with the reader being seen as positioned as a form of subject at different points in the text. Again, the view that we bring to the analysis concerning overdetermination of meaning in the text allows us to see multiple subject positions as formed simultaneously and in contradiction to one another. The positions that are constituted for the addressee may be complementary on occasion, but language also routinely disrupts our sense of self, and we anxiously and perpetually smooth it over to keep ourselves together. Psychoanalytic discourse analysis opens the contradictions in subject positions, and so too the contradictions in the subject caught in the text.

The third assumption concerns the construction of the meaning in the text, as a relatively enduring semantic structure that 'holds' the reader in position. While there is undoubtedly the reconstruction of sense moment by moment on the different occasions the text is read, there are also patterns of meaning, the discourses as sets of statements that constitute objects, that return to the reader. These patterns are relayed in the wider culture that hosts the text and the reader, and replayed as the organized tacit conditions for sense that makes it possible for the text to work. The kinds of reader or 'subject' constituted in the culture (subjects schooled in talk of the unconscious, infantile sexuality and suchlike) come to the text prepared to read particular constellations of signs (keywords, turns of phrase, and allusions to what is 'other' to the text) that have been fabricated as part of the underlying common sense of the culture (Parker, 1993). Here it useful to read the culture alongside the text as composed of 'discursive complexes' which relay meaning and specify subject positions. The step that we take into an analysis of discourse as a patterned field of signification as well as an accomplishment of individual speakers then leads us to take seriously cultural resources that individuals draw upon to fashion themselves as competent selves. Psychoanalysis is a potent element in the discourse of selfhood in Western culture, and so discourse analysis should itself draw upon that resource in the research process.

Method

Three aspects of psychoanalytic method as it pertains to discourse research can be identified, and these will be employed during the analysis of text in question in this chapter.

The first concerns the sensitivity of the researcher, and the ways in which the subjective resources of the reader are brought to bear on the material. These resources are structured, in the process of a psychoanalytic reading, by transference (what is brought to the unconscious relationship the reader has to the text by the text, and its host culture) and counter-transference (what is brought to the text by the reader, and the culture they inhabit). The subjectivity of the reader is mobilized by this dual relationship and gives rise to certain responses (which emerge in the course of the reading) and inhibitions (which obscure a relationship with the intersubjective field that constitutes a text within a symbolic community). It is easier, of course, to display and reflect upon responses than it is to do so with inhibitions, but the analysis can attempt to keep present to attention the ways in which 'absences' and 'otherness' to the text are systematically structured. The symptomatic reading that results will take the form of systematic speculation around the points where the text does not make 'sense'.

The second aspect concerns the form of the reading, and the ways in which psychoanalytic concepts are brought to bear on the text to open up the semantic (and so, also, discursively constituted psychic) mechanisms that organize it. Psychoanalysis is treated here as a methodological vocabulary which is deployed to restructure the text in terms that render unconscious defences and libidinal forces meaningful as linguistic patterns. The aim here is not to uncover such defences or forces in the 'author' of the text (though an imagined author may be produced at some point to facilitate the reading), but to focus on the patterns in the text, in the relationship it provokes with the reader and in the relationship it reproduces (as mediator) between the reader and culture (and so wider systems of discourse). At each point of focus psychoanalytic vocabulary reframes and elaborates what may be going on. In the case of the patterns in the text psychoanalytic terms can be kept at a distance (as if they simply existed in the material), but the relationship between the text and reader and the relationship it re-marks between the reader and the culture includes us (and the overall analytic frame is again that of transference and counter-transference).

The third aspect concerns the way forms of culture are represented in the text, and in particular the way in which psychoanalytic culture is transmitted in discourse (directly or indirectly, deliberately or unintentionally). A reading of culture as a meshwork of discourses which can be analytically decomposed needs to be connected here with a cultural history of the different forms of subjectivity (and the emphasis for these purposes is on psychoanalytic subjectivity) that are constituted for readers now. Psychoanalytic notions which thread through contemporary Western culture are located in the text here as 'discursive complexes' which simultaneously carry discourses and elaborate sets of subject positions for actors in the text and for readers of the text. Discursive complexes are patterns of meaning that systematically form objects and subjects, but their internal structure derives from psychoanalytic discourse. Notions of childhood 'complex', the 'ego' and the 'unconscious' together with the panoply of strategies that one may use to reflect upon these objects ('acting out', 'repetition', 'working through', etc.) circulate as elements of self-understanding in Western culture. A psychoanalytic discourse reading does not treat these notions as given, but looks to the ways in which texts reproduce such categories, and reproduce subjects who can make sense of the texts that hold them.

The text

The back of the toothpaste tube contains, in blue type, the following instructions:

DIRECTIONS FOR USE

Choose a children's brush that has a small head and add a pea-sized amount of Punch and Judy toothpaste. To teach your child to clean teeth, stand behind and place your hand under the child's chin to tilt head back and see mouth. Brush both sides of teeth as well as tops. Brush after breakfast and last thing at night. Supervise the brushing of your child's teeth until the age of eight. If your child is taking fluoride treatment, seek professional advice concerning daily intake.

Contains 0.8% Sodium Monofluorophosphate

The tube is small, like other tubes of toothpaste for children, and white. The front of the tube has, in large red letters with blue shadow, the legend 'PUNCH and JUDY TOOTHPASTE'. The manufacturer's name ('Maws') is above in silhouette on a blue background, and there is a line below, in red, which reads, 'Children's Toothpaste with Fluoride'. A border of red strawberries (with blue leaves) circles each end of the tube, and eight more strawberries are dotted around on the front. There is a picture on the front of the tube, and again next to instructions, of the head of Punch smiling and holding a red toothbrush in his mouth. He wears a blue ruff around his neck and a red frill around his one visible hand (which holds the brush).

Analysis

A preliminary analysis (Banister *et al.*, 1994), following methodological steps outlined in Parker (1992a) which trace the clusters of objects, subjects and social relationships that are specified in the text, concluded with an outline of four discourses. These were: 'rationalist' – in which the ability to follow procedures ('directions for use') requires choices of implement and judgement of amount ('small head' and 'pea-sized amount') and is predicated on recognition of appropriate authority in health care (following 'directions' and seeking 'professional advice'); 'familial' – in which ownership ('your child') runs alongside supervision and continuous care (the assumption that the child is present each breakfast and 'last thing at night') and is framed by the image of bad parenting (the figure of 'Punch and Judy'); 'developmental–educational' – in which the teaching of the child (parental activity) precedes supervision (the child's still tutored but self-governed activity) and then reaches an identifiable stage as a developmental milestone (the 'age of eight'); and 'medical' – in which the process of using the toothpaste is necessarily linked to hygiene (brushing after meals), professional supervision ('fluoride treatment') and the specification of ingestion and chemical composition of substances ('daily intake', '0.8% Sodium Monofluorophosphate').

An essential part of discourse analysis is the production of a 'critical distance' between the reader and the text so that one is able to ask what collections of relationships and theories of self must obtain for this material to make sense. That step back can go as far as to throw into question the material conditions that would be necessary for the text to 'work'. There are, for example, background assumptions about the nature of memory and the activity of teethcleaning as a private activity for which tutoring (through the medium of the text) is appropriate, and the text operates as a practice in a world of toothbrushes, running water and electric light (to see the teeth last thing at night). The psychoanalytic construction, function and variation in the text can also be approached through exploring the conditions of possibility for these notions to work in this culture as conditions of possibility for psychoanalysis itself. One can ask how such aspects of the world (privatized hygiene, personalized advice and self-regulation) also incite forms of behaviour, experience and reflection that are amenable to psychotherapeutic, psychoanalytic talk. Two further methodological points of focus can be illustrated here.

The first concerns 'feeling', forms of inchoate response to the text which cannot be tied one to one to terms or phrases. Psychoanalysis is centrally concerned with the organization of affect, and the analysis of meaning, which discourse analysis is capable of addressing, needs now to be supplemented with an analysis of the 'drives' in the text. This is not to say that actual libidinal forces pulsate through the text, but that meanings are structured such that they operate as dynamic, and then for the reader as psychodynamic, forces. The case in point here is how one would be able to capture the violence in the text. An activity is represented here in which the child is physically restrained while a cleaning implement is inserted in the mouth. There is powerful affect running alongside meaning, and it is helpful to attend to our 'emotional response' to the text, to images in the text here as varieties of affect produced in discourse. The violence is distributed around certain oppositions, which are then mapped onto subjects (the parent and the child) specified in the text.

The second methodological point of focus concerns the elaboration of oppositions, and their particular relationship to domination and compliance (and to force and resistance). It is useful to attend to forms of splitting in the text, with the production of oppositions which can be read deconstructively to open up the text as a cultural practice, for to open the text up in this way reveals the operations of power that privilege certain practices. This point extends a 'deconstructive' reading of texts (Parker, 1988). In this case the pair 'adult–child' is mapped onto 'reality–pleasure' (ensuring hygiene versus enjoying the taste), 'knowledge–naivety' (following instructions versus being supervised) and 'work–play' (teaching the task versus consuming jolly toothpaste), and – this is where the violence is reproduced – onto the opposition 'active–passive'. The activity and passivity in the text are also replayed in the relationship of the text to reader, with the recipient of advice subordinate to the addressor (as subject supposed to know) and professional (in alliance with the addressor).

These considerations are now of assistance in building upon the initial description of the four discourses to produce a psychoanalytic reading, and thus to the elaboration of 'discursive complexes'. Discursive complexes as, simultaneously, forms of discourse and relays of psychoanalytic subjectivity can be used as analytic devices to connect the material in the text with broader cultural patterns. Discursive complexes take the form of psychoanalytic concepts, but should be understood as socially constructed, symbolically maintained, not as reflections of individual psychic states (though it will indeed be the case that an individual 'subjected' to such symbolic material is constituted as a 'psychoanalytic subject' for whom such a mode of interpretation will then make sense).

The Oedipal triangle

Although the Oedipus complex is so important in psychoanalysis, Freud declined to call it a 'complex' until 1910, fourteen years after he first puzzled over the fraught connection the infant has with the first love object (in Western nuclear families, usually the mother) and then with the first threat (usually the father, as the third term in the relationship). The image of the Oedipal triangle structures the internal psychic economy of the infant, and as a discursive form it both structures and disrupts the opposition in this text between 'adult' and 'child'. The repression of gender as a category in this text, marked by the absence of gendered possessive pronouns ('to clean teeth', 'sides of teeth'), also raises a question about the gender of each of the participants in the scene enacted here. Gender is absent in cultural conditions which are saturated by gender. Why? And why should the relationship between addressee and infant ('your child') be violent, violating?

The clue which solves both questions is the motif of Punch and Judy, and that motif is relayed into the text by the figure of Punch. Punch and Judy function here as exemplars of aberrant abusive parents, and Punch alone operates in a double position as representative of the Law (the third term with the stick, which in this case is also the toothbrush which he holds in his mouth) and as violator of the Law (with the stick as the weapon with which he batters the child, and Judy). Žižek (1991), employing psychoanalytic theory, has pointed out that the Law always produces excess, supplementary unlawful violence as a condition for the Law to function. A supplement father in the Punch and Judy narrative, the policeman, then enforces the Law as good parental figure, and a further splitting in the narrative produces the crocodile (who traditionally, it can be noted, has big white teeth) as the excess of violence which threatens all three in the triangle. The 'adult–child' couple, then, is overlaid by a particular affective shape which is given by the discursive complex of the Oedipal triangle, and it is then possible to account for the splitting between the activities of (health) care in the text and the (regulative) violence of the text as a screen for that which is excluded (Oedipus).

The reality principle

In the Punch and Judy narrative which both frames the activity specified in this text and functions as a warning as to the characteristics of parents who would fail to follow these instructions, Punch is the figure who shouts 'That's the way to do it!' Punch initiates the infant, and the audience (of children) into a form of violent (ir)rationality, a surplus of enjoyment in the puppet narrative which is also, for the battered baby, and Judy, beyond the pleasure principle. The discursive complex of the reality principle is useful here to capture the opposition 'reality–pleasure' that underpins this text. Mouth hygiene is on the side of reality, and enjoyment of the taste on the side of pleasure, but the opposition carries much more besides. The opposition comes all the closer to psychoanalytic notions of reality (the social) and pleasure (the body) when it is mapped onto other oppositions that are operating in this material. In this discursive complex, the irrational and the rational are also mapped onto the relationship between the body and language.

The untutored child is physically restrained, and the body is moved into positions that will facilitate the eventual supervision (as a moment of transition between the pleasure of the infant and the reality of the adult world) and then self-governance of the child (after eight) who is able to 'clean teeth'. While the child's body is physically positioned, the adult (the addressee) is positioned as a rational subject through language. The adult is constituted as a being who can be addressed through language (in this case, written instructions), and the relationship with authority (the addressor, as 'subject supposed to know', the imaginary author of the instructions) is symbolically mediated. The seeking of 'professional advice' will also be carried out through the medium of language. In this opposition, then, the body is irrational (to be tutored) child, and the mind is rational (to be addressed) adult. The opposition also encourages a particular common-sense 'theoretical' reflection – that which one finds in Althusser's (1971) attempt to produce a psychoanalytic account of ideology for example – on the way in which one is inducted into society as a physical practice, something that can be set in contrast to the ways in which one then reflects upon society as a linguistic achievement.

Enigmatic signifiers

The opposition between the adult and the child also carries a contrast between knowledge and naivety, in which one member of the pair is able to follow instructions, and the other follows the route to knowledge through supervision from ignorance. The naivety of the child is also important to psychoanalysis, which adds a paradoxical twist to images of childhood innocence. For while the child is seen as outside the social order, innocent of the nature of reality (and following the pleasure principle) it is in its nature (also following the pleasure principle) to be driven to know. What the child experiences of sexuality, for example, is not yet linked with what it is possible to know, and what it is possible to know of sexuality as adult knowledge will both articulate and transform what the child once experienced. The paradox of the innocent child surrounded by, and affected by, adult mysteries which it cannot yet comprehend can be grasped, picking up a term used by the analyst Laplanche (1989), through the discursive complex of 'enigmatic signifiers'.

In this text, however, apart from questions of sexuality (obscured and operative through the absence of gender), there are questions of power and violence; that which is incomprehensible to the child (as physical restraint) will be rendered meaningful as the child reaches a certain developmental point. Here the penetration of the child's body (their mouth) is linked to a form of knowledge (and the practice of a form of knowledge). The description here is technical, positions the child as an object, and the parent maintains the child as if they were a mechanism (which then, at some developmental point, becomes sentient). Reading the text through the figure of enigmatic signifiers also throws further light on the riddle of the 'violence' of the text. The activity of brushing the interior of the mouth after restraining the head is a scene in which an adult with power gazes upon and acts upon the child. There is then a resonance between objectification of the child (as innocent object with the wish to become subject) and accounts of objectification in pornography. The fluoride is also marked as an object to be inserted, as 'intake', as a substance to be placed into the child, and the toothbrush functions metaphorically as a 'speculum' (a device for observing the interior of the body and producing knowledge) constituting the space (the mouth, the tutored child) from which discourse will one day emerge.

Sites of resistance

It would be possible to provide a quasi-Foucauldian reading of the text as a sealed world in which processes of regulation and surveillance constitute all the limits and interior space of what it is possible to do and know. However, the opposition 'work–play', the contrast between the teaching of the task and the consumption of the jolly toothpaste, opens a space for manoeuvre, a space that a psychoanalytic reading should exploit. There is a carnivalesque resistance in the form of Punch and Judy. Rather like the anarchic vision of 'schizophrenia' in Deleuze and Guattari's (1977) *Anti-Oedipus*, Punch and Judy are provoked as a condition of the text, and to work efficiently to support the text as instruction they must be limited, bounded, contained, so that their subversive potential cannot be realized. They are produced to the limit (and to regulate the limits) of what is rational (against the irrational). The text is part of a machinery of desire (and, for Deleuze and Guattari, of capitalism); it incites play to sell a commodity and then turns that into work to reproduce the relations of power that make such commodities possible.

What makes it possible for this text to work is that the child (and the reader positioned as a child, in identification with the child, as they buy the text) is lured into the scene. The subjugation and training of the child is facilitated by the images of play, and the reader is drawn into the text as a player with power, but not in command of the apparatus of power (that is, the powerful subject is also subject to the power). However, a Foucauldian account of power is always also an account of resistance, and to speak of a discursive complex of 'sites of resistance' allows us to elaborate how that resistance may operate in the psychic economy of readers. The very process of luring the child (and adult identified as child) into the text provokes the fantasy of disruption, the transformation of the supervision scene into play. Punch, for example, is the Law and the disruptor of the Law, and at the very moment that he exercises the Law to the full he throws it into question. This reading of the text also throws it into question, and psychoanalysis, as a theory of resistance, opens a space from which we may think against the text, mark ourselves as different to the subject positions it creates for us and within us.

Discussion

Some further consideration should now be given to method, and in particular to the cultural location of psychoanalysis as a lens through which to view subjectivity and as a vocabulary by means of which a reading of a text can be articulated. It would be possible to argue (as many psychoanalytic practitioners and theorists do) that psychoanalysis provides a vivid insight into the psychic economy of the paraphernalia of material culture because it accurately addresses the internal forces and relations of the individual human subjects that produce (or write) and consume (or read) it. No such claim is being made here, and if anything, the opposite. For research subjectivity and psychoanalytic structures are seen in this chapter as constituted by the culture they inhabit. That is, transference, counter-transference, defence mechanisms and libidinal forces are themselves seen as semantic forms which circulate through 'discursive complexes'. In this case, therefore, the reading of a text which is ostensibly so apparently innocent of the unconscious has to be 're-read' as it is reconstituted as a piece of material in a psychoanalytic culture.

This chapter has employed psychoanalytic notions in the broadest sense to elaborate a discourse-analytic reading. Although there has been reference to particular theories within the Freudian and post-Freudian tradition, my concern has been with the most general culturally available analytic images of the family, rationality, curiosity and resistance. The Lacanian tradition as been particularly useful in this reading, with the work of Althusser (1971), Deleuze and Guattari (1977), Laplanche (1989) and Žižek (1991) throwing light on the work of ideology, resistance, knowledge and power. It is important to note that the ways we can reflect on the operations of this text as researchers are also conditioned by the very forms of discourse that inhabit the text. Here, then, we should be aware of assumptions in the Lacanian tradition that frame our interpretation. In the case of the infant being inducted physically into language and the adult reproducing that practice through the medium of language, for example, we should take care to see this as an account of ideology, not necessarily as an accurate explication of its nature. This theoretical, and psychoanalytic, reflection is expressed, among other places, in Althusser's (1971) writing which counterposes the induction of the subject into ideology as a practice (of 'ideological state apparatuses' such as the school) to the theoretical practice and scientific reflection upon ideology as conducted through the symbolic order. Similar points could be made about the specific cultural location of Deleuze and Guattari's celebration of 'schizophrenia' as resistance, Laplanche's description of the child puzzling over adult sensual knowledge and Žižek's view of the Law as always provoking its hideous reverse.

The analytic device of the 'discursive complex' is used to provide a more thoroughly embedded notion of subject position than that offered by, for example, Davies and Harré (1990). The position taken by the subject is not adopted moment by moment as an individual engages with the material, but is discursively given to the reader. This does not mean that the reader is passive, but that certain conditions of possibility for the text also permit certain relationships to be formed within the text and, from within other texts, towards and against it. The engagement with any text is always an engagement from within discourse, and the task of a discourse-analytic reading is to engage in a way that lays bare the work of ideology and the plays of power, the unravelling of ideology and the spaces of resistance (Parker, 1992a).

In the research process the subject positions, and general issues of activity and passivity in the text, are compounded by the process of reading as the struggle for mastery over the text. Different forms of identification are produced in the text, as actors in the text operate as exemplars of subject positions that can be adopted or refused. The analysis has adopted a subject position (of researcher) which also speaks about what is excluded (repressed), and an active position is taken in relation to regions of the symbolic order that are usually closed. The subject position of the researcher can then also be drawn out using psychoanalytic theory. There are risks. In this case the gaze of the psy-complex (the array of theories and practices that comprise the discipline of academic and professional psychology) is reproduced in the activity of the parent regulating, through the supervisory gaze, the child. The developmental–educational discourse that runs through the text is interwoven with images of the rational individual, the family and medicine, and this cluster of discourses reinforces the power of psychology as a 'regime of truth' (Banister *et al.*, 1994). The researcher using psychoanalytic theory as described in this chapter now gazes upon the text, and upon the parent and child, in a metaposition that is actually still of a piece with the activities of the psy-complex. The regulation of children is a condition for the psy-complex, and it is important to remember that it is also a condition for psychoanalysis (and now for us) as part of (and other of) the psy-complex.

5 Against discursive imperialism, empiricism and constructionism

with Erica Burman

> The ways in which discourse research can open up texts and produce innovative analysis is evident from the preceding chapters. These next two chapters are much more critical of discourse analysis. This chapter was written jointly with Erica Burman following a conference we organized for the Discourse Unit in 1991, and so you can see that the worries we both have articulated in the last twenty years were apparent even then. We identify thirty-two problems with discourse analysis in this paper. The first six problems were actually raised by participants in the conference (by Ros Gill, Phil Macnaghten, Deborah Marks, Harriet Marshall, Paul Stenner, Bianca Raabe and Sue Widdicombe).
>
> At the conference were visitors from Puerto Rico who had been working with discursive ideas in the field of cultural and media studies; two, Heidi Figueroa Sarriera and María Milagros López (who has since died), drew attention to more of the problems which we pick up in our review here. The critical reflexive commentary on discourse analysis from this early date is testimony to the hope that the approach would break from mainstream psychology – from the 'old paradigm' – and the worry that an alternative method could be absorbed and neutralized by the discipline.
>
> We outline problems that have been identified in current practice, problems in the framework as a whole, problems that flow from attempts to escape these issues, problems which arise, as a consequence, in teaching the approach and problems attending the wholesale application of the approach to everything in the

> world. We conclude with some questions about the way forward for discourse analysis. Many contributors to the conference went on to do interesting critical work which eventually moved on from discourse analysis altogether, a step that we perhaps now need to take.

The development of a newly arrived approach will meet, as a matter of course, objections from the host discipline, and some of the drawbacks to discourse analysis also resonate with some of the concerns of the mainstream in psychology. Six issues immediately emerge, and some of these will undoubtedly appear in criticisms of discourse-analytic studies a researcher may produce.

Six problems of method

The first three problems are ones that will be relevant to most types of research currently carried out in psychology.

1. Discourse analysis is, as many new researchers often point out, very labour-intensive. The task of trawling through pages of interview transcript (not to mention the transcribing of the material in the first place if interviews or recorded discussions are used) is a tedious and time-consuming one. In this respect, discourse analysis, as with many other varieties of qualitative research is usually *more* difficult than positivist number crunching (Banister *et al.*, 1994).
2. It is difficult to determine whether the different repertoires or discourses are present in the text as discrete phenomena, or whether the changes in context are responsible for changes in meaning. It is sometimes difficult to determine that *different* discourses are at work. Some researchers are also worried about the idea that we could imagine that we were simply 'letting discourses emerge'. Discourses are not already there waiting to be found but emerge (as much through our work of reading as from the text).
3. It is difficult to move from a specific text, from a particular usage, to a wider context, and it is frustrating to feel that we cannot make broad empirical generalizations; there is thus what some see as a failure to theorize universal processes, and some researchers are thus also unhappy that discourse analysts do not usually give any indication of the frequency of usage of rhetorical devices.

These concerns flowing from the standpoint of traditional psychology can be augmented by three problems that express the frustration of analysts wanting to do critical work, and wanting discourse analysis to be a critical approach.

4   The analyst is often restricted, for practical reasons (having to fit a research project into a limited space or time), to the confines of the text. It is often the case that there is little opportunity for consideration of large-scale political consequences of the repertoires in the material being studied. While this could be seen simply as a problem of reductionism hitting social psychologists again (Billig, 1976), there are particular ironies, and issues to be confronted when the repertoires have been understood as having their source in the surrounding social and political context.

5   The traditional complaint that discourse research does not provide a sufficiently rigorous methodology, in which the reader is satisfied that the analysis has produced the only possible reading, is mirrored in the complaint that the analysis tempts us into trying to close the text to alternative readings. To introduce closure is to do violence to the variety of possible interpretations that could be given of the text when it comes to life in a discourse-analytic reading (and to the variety of possible meanings which were present to those who once wrote or spoke the text).

6   There is a further problem here which follows from that of bringing about closure, which is to do with the power of the analyst to impose meanings upon some else's text. There are ethical problems in having power and control over other people's words, and this raises the issue of experts legitimating already-existing discourse. These are issues of power and morality in research. As part of a movement in research that rejected the dehumanizing methods of traditional psychology, it is right that discourse analysts should consider the power of the researcher as expert, and the exercise of power is all the worse when covered over by the illusion of democratization and the disingenuous fantasy of empowerment.

Are there more problems that threaten to enmire the researcher? There are.

Six further problems of method

We can supplement these six issues with a further six identified, in a commentary on discourse-analytic research in Britain, by Figueroa and López

(1991). These problems appear, at first glance, to be of a different type from those raised so far, for they look as if they could be solved (if the researcher did the research properly). This appearance, however, is deceptive since these are problems of another order that demand critical and challenging reflection on the parameters of the research framework and process.

7. There is a serious danger of attempting to prevent the analysis of grammatical constructions from leading to an analysis of the social relations implied by discursive forms. Some varieties of discourse analysis (particularly that influenced by post-structuralism) do deliberately focus on social relations and 'subject positions' in discourse, but even here the temptation for the researcher is to simply identify rhetorical devices (or repertoires, or discourses), and the report of the analysis neglects the way that language always does things, always reproduces or transforms social relationships. The analysis threatens to avoid the 'performative' aspect of language (Bowers and Iwi, 1991). The production of different social relations in different discourses is overdetermined by the production of different social relations in different texts.

8. Not only are there different social relations set up in different discourses, but different types of text work in different ways (they are accessible to different readers, and are read according to their form and context). There is a risk of taking what one imagines to be the 'method' of discourse analysis and applying it to all texts, without bearing these differences in text in mind. This would become particularly important if the framework was used to analyse texts which were not written or spoken (art, filmic or music texts). The fact that the discourse-analytic strand of psychology has tended to focus on spoken or written texts suggests that this is an issue that we are evading rather than resolving.

9. A related problem here, and a symptom of confusion over competing styles of analysis, is that of using such terms as 'discourse', 'text', 'narrative', 'theme' and 'story' as if they were interchangeable. The meanings and uses of these particular terms need to be carefully specified.

The next three problems concern deeper issues to do with the overarching analytic framework and commitments of the researcher.

10. There is a danger of idealism, not only with reference to the problems of relativism and voluntarism (which we discuss below), but also in the attention only to language at the expense of an attention to the materiality of power. Although power is certainly (re)produced in discourse, power is also at work in the structural position of people when they are not speaking. Power relations endure when the text stops (Parker,

80   *Against discursive imperialism etc.*

1992a). In part, the reluctance of psychologists to engage with the issue of power in a systematic way is a result of the focus historically of the discipline of psychology upon the individual. Other disciplines are left to deal with societal factors.

11   There is a serious separate issue here in the isolation of psychology from other disciplines, and the attempt to confine analysis to psychology. This is manifested in the problem of competence, the reluctance to address the degree to which the cultural competence of the reader is necessary. Some awareness of cultural trends, of allusions to political and social developments, is essential for a discourse analysis to work. If you do not know what a text is referring to, you cannot produce a reading.

12   The problem of the (lack of) cultural knowledge of a reader is echoed by another problem which is that of the position of the reader as researcher. Critical analysts of discourse have pointed to the problem of power relations between researcher and researched and the ethics of imposing meanings, but in the process of reflection we also have to be aware of the way in which analysts are not only readers but also producers of discourse. They are implicated in the production of the forms of knowledge they describe. To offer a reading of a text is, in some manner or other, to reproduce or transform it.

And another two problems of method: interpretive vigilance and ambivalence

Two further points identified by Figueroa and López (1991) should be included, for they pertain to the overall state of discourse-analytic research.

13   There is in much discourse-analytic research a sensitivity to the way language is gendered, but there is still a question as to how what Figueroa and López call the 'interpretive vigilance' exercised by feminists over readings could be extended to include an attention to other varieties of oppression. Despite the panic (particularly in the United States) from the 1990s over 'political correctness' in language (Robbins, 1991), we still do believe that a moral/political sensitivity to the way oppression is maintained in language is required of discourse analysts (who are supposed to be aware of social relations in texts).

14   An ambivalence (and we use the word advisedly) over the use of psychoanalytic concepts is a problem. This is not so much of a problem because there are forms of discourse analysis appearing which use psychoanalysis (Walkerdine, 1988; Hollway, 1989; Parker, 1992a). Rather, the (more complex) problem here is that discourse analysts

are still sometimes pursuing their texts in a way that is suspicious of what is manifest, and looking to hidden meanings. We use terms, for example, like 'overdetermination' (to refer to the multiple causation of semantic phenomena) and at the same time seem wary of making the connections with psychoanalysis, a 'hermeneutics of suspicion' par excellence.

The fourteen problems we have outlined so far have already touched on more fundamental problems than those pertaining to the refinement of technique. Now we want to pursue these deeper issues further. We will organize our reservations about discourse analysis by using the notions of 'empiricism' and 'constructionism', for it appears to us that these terms are not in a type of opposition in which one is right and one is wrong, but are twin problems. The rush to constructionism that discourse-analytic research hastens is not a solution to the empiricism of orthodox psychology (an empiricism that discourse analysts wish to escape).

Empiricism and constructionism

Psychology traditionally adopts an empiricist approach to human action. This means not only that the discipline favours empirical work, and would like to check theories against the world (and we would agree that empirical studies are necessary), but rather it means that it adopts the view that the only knowledge worth having (or that it is *possible* to have) is derived from the prediction and control of (probabilistic) laws of behaviour. This refusal to acknowledge the role of theory in the production of knowledge (except when it is viewed as 'bias'), and a fetish with the collection of what it thinks are neutral facts, is empiricism. Harré makes the point that the refusal of empiricists to look deeper than the surface, and the compulsive measurement of what is going on at the surface, is closely connected to an inability to cope with uncertainty: 'The more powerful and speculative, the deeper do our theories purport to go in the exploration of nature, the less can we be certain of their correctness' (Harré, 1981: 9). The only way that psychologists can be certain about things is to cling to what they can measure. Empiricism is bound up with an obsession with truth.

The shift to discourse analysis is ostensibly part of a movement away from empiricism towards social constructionism (Gergen, 1985). Social constructionism encompasses a range of approaches in psychology which share the view that our knowledge about ourselves is culturally bounded, and that different cultural (and sub-cultural) systems entail different psychologies, sometimes called 'indigenous psychologies' (Heelas and Lock, 1981). The traditional empiricist psychologists are ridiculed for their preoccupation with truth, and constructionism instead looks to a more open analysis of the way psychology changes from culture to culture, from historical period to historical period, and the way our knowledge of that psychology will necessarily also change. There is a profound connection between psychology and culture, and we have to take care not to misunderstand how that connection works and, in particular, in which direction that connection operates. Empiricist psychologists might go so far as to acknowledge that psychological theory seeps out into culture and affects it (and this undoubtedly does happen), but social constructionists (and we would count ourselves among them on this point) would say that it is more the case that culture contains particular distinct types of psychology which seep into and mould the discipline of 'psychology'.

It is all the more paradoxical and disturbing, then, to find discourse analysis in practice slipping from social constructionism back to empiricism. We have two suggestions as to why this should be, but we want first to offer examples, describe some of the problems in discourse analysis, that are connected to this slide to empiricism. The set of problems here occurs in the teaching of the approach.

Back to empiricism: a further seven problems

By 'teaching' we mean all attempts to persuade someone that discourse analysis is a 'good thing' and to explain why. One of the worrying aspects of discourse analysis is the abstract character of the debates. The theoretical framework is not easy to understand, and as such it is open to the charge of elitism when we elaborate an analysis which defies simple exposition and which explicitly resists generalized description or easy 'how-to-do-it' rules. What we want to deal with here now is how discourse analysis can function in ways that are compatible with traditional empiricist research through our efforts to make it more accessible.

Reactions of those new to discourse analysis is broadly of two sorts, and their reactions constitute two further problems.

15 For a first group without a political commitment or framework, the approach is either incomprehensible or irrelevant. The only way to deal with this confusion is for them to learn 'how to do it' and so slip into an alternative, and more dangerous position, in which they treat the analytic style as applicable to the deconstruction of anything and everything.
16 In contrast, a discourse framework holds an implicit appeal to a second group, those who already have some political sense and can recognize its relevance and scope. They know already that language contains and

reinforces ideology. Those who are already politicized do discourse analysis without knowing that they have done it, or what it is that they have done. They have simply generated the analysis that makes sense to them in a fairly atheoretical, but politically informed, way. Then, to this second group, the relativism ushered in by some aspects of reflexivity is frustrating since it supports the prevailing taboo on politics in the academe. It then becomes a route from politics to opportunism.

These two problems in the reactions of those we teach pale into insignificance when we turn to consider the problems we reproduce when we teach it. We will identify five problems here.

17 The first is that of treating it as a value-free technology. The easiest (and safest) way to teach discourse analysis is to present it as a technology, as a theory-free method or as a tool to do research. This encourages the view that discourse analysis can be 'applied', that it is an 'it' (Potter *et al.*, 1990). The project to 'identify' discourses not only sets up a divide between method and interpretation that flies in the face of an emphasis on reflexivity in the new wave of anti-positivist psychology, but through this it also sets up a position of separation between the discourse analyst and the text. In the activity of determining the scope of, and terms within, discourses we imagine that the boundaries which we are setting are necessary in order to make the work manageable. But in doing this we are also subscribing to a fantasy of non-involvement in the material we are analysing not dissimilar from the traditional methodologies we turned to discourse analysis to escape.

18 We are also ineluctably caught in the trap of reifying the discourse. Further empiricist dangers lurk within the tendency of discourse analysis towards abstraction. Depicting discourses as abstract and autonomous meaning systems that float above social practice, or that constitute social practice in mysterious ways, can work to remove discourse analysis from the realms of everyday life. It becomes an academic pursuit, and so we are continually subject to the charge of reifying discourse (Potter *et al.*, 1990). Additional difficulties are involved in specifying the relationship between discourses and the social practices that give rise to them. Just as empiricism constructs its model of the world, treats what it measures as the real (by the process of 'operationalizing' its concepts), so discourse analysis may be in danger of mistaking discourse as the sum total, rather than the manifestation of, structural relationships.

19 Although we want to show that discourse research produces more interesting analyses than traditional psychology, we cannot pretend that we

are able to 'discover' things in the way that the rest of the discipline thinks it does, and in our attempt to flee from this we encounter the problem of banality. If discourse analysis tends towards overcomplexity and abstraction, it also encounters difficulties in dealing with the familiar. Perhaps we could justify the (imaginary) separation between researcher and text as working to 'defamiliarize', or make strange, everyday practices in which we are ordinarily embedded in order to more clearly investigate their rules and structures. We could see it as a sort of critical-analytic ethnography; discourse analysis tries to elucidate webs of meaning, and the relations and consequences of competing meaning frameworks. But one problem we encounter is that we find it difficult to classify or categorize the seemingly 'obvious'. The analysis can seem like 'common sense', a charge which echoes popular, and well-founded, resistance to mainstream psychology.

20 The next problem in teaching is where we encounter once again, in a modified form, the perils of reductionism. In this respect, discourse analysis has clear continuities with empiricism, and this continuity lies in its reductionist tendencies. This reductionism can be either of the psychological or sociological variety, and here the problem appears as one of voluntarism (or, to counter that, crude anti-humanism). The explicit or implicit identification of intentional agents manipulating discourses or engaging in discursive strategies (because there is an inadequately theorized notion of resistance and discursive position) smacks of a voluntarism that tends also towards cognitivism. On the other hand, the conception of discourses as if they were 'tectonic plates' whose clashes constitute subjectivity can present so distributed a notion of power that there is no room for agency, thus also lapsing into mechanistic explanation (Potter *et al.*, 1990). The problem here is macro-reduction to discursive structures which complements micro-reduction to individual agency, giving rise to a different, but equally unhelpful, illusory or limited scope for struggle.

21 Finally, we have to resort too often (in our desire to be clear in our account of how discourse analysis could be done) to a temporality and a historicism. The elaboration of a range of positions in relation to language (even when it is seen as social practice) does not necessarily imply a commitment to change those positions. There is a danger that in delineating the structure of (albeit historically constituted) discursive relations we implicitly overemphasize the static features of discursive relations. This is an effect which, paradoxically, threatens to reinstate discourses as being as universal, fixed and timeless. It is necessary for discourse analysis to theorize fluctuations and transformations in discursive relations to ward off a reading of them as unchanging.

From constructionism to empiricism

We suggest that there are two causes of this last cluster of seven problems. The first is to do with the location of this research in traditional academic institutions. There is still the question of how the rules of institutions (and the career ambitions and investments of participants who have to work within those rules) deform critical thought, and ensure that radical work plays the game. In many respects, our problems in relaying discourse work to others is a function of that context. The second cause is to do with the nature of contemporary culture, and the transition, in some sectors (particularly some academic sectors) of culture from 'modernity' to 'postmodernity' (Lyotard, 1979/1984; Burman, 1992a; Parker, 1992b). Two important characteristics of the postmodern turn in culture are the shift from depth to surface and the shift from a belief in truth to a celebration of the impossibility of truth, to uncertainty. This double shift, the flight from depth and truth, is, we believe, the cultural setting for discourse analysis. And, in the way that changes in culture always provide the conditions of possibility for changes in (the discipline of) psychology, this setting encourages a variety of discourse analysis which is simultaneously hostile to notions of depth (as empiricism always was) and happy with uncertainty (which empiricism traditionally was not). Discourse analysis, then, risks mutating into a form of postmodern constructionist empiricism.

Empiricism and imperialism: three more problems

The next twist, and it is exacerbated when culture itself increasingly appears to take a postmodern form (that is, it appears to be only surface and to be revelling in uncertainty) is that discourse analysis turns into a form of academic imperialism. This happens when it is used to give sense to all everyday discursive clashes. That everyday clashes of meaning can be informed by discourse analysis is clear. The issue is whether this is always helpful. When is discourse analysis useful, and when is it useless?

These three problems are as follows, and they each revolve around the slogan 'you don't have to be a discourse analyst to see that . . .'.

22 The first concerns the question as to whether discourse research is taken to be applicable to an issue because it is 'interesting', or whether it should be applicable because the issue is embedded in a particular and significant context. Is discourse analysis the goal, or should we rather be using it strategically (with other goals in mind). For example, the claim by some male lecturers that there is no moral problem in sleeping with students is often justified by an appeal to the liberal notion of 'choice'. The student in higher education is an adult, so the claim goes,

86 *Against discursive imperialism etc.*

and so it is up to her to 'choose'. That this position obscures (excuses, and abuses) power is a point that a discourse analyst could easily miss. An analysis of the connections between notions of choice used here and free-market images of choice used to justify inequality in economic relationships (between owner and worker, producer and consumer) might be seen merely as 'interesting', and it would skirt the real issue. The notion of 'choice' is used here rhetorically to hide power, and you don't have to be a discourse analyst to see that.

23 A second, related, issue is whose analysis we are dealing with. This sets up further questions of practice in terms of the positions the discourse analyst constructs. The current plans for 'community treatment' of people who have experienced mental distress are interpreted by self-advocacy groups as thinly disguised devices for their regulation and control (e.g. BNAP, 1988; Lawson, 1988; LAMHA, 1988). Here, the analysis offered by the group we would presumably want to support coincides with that offered by post-structuralists (e.g. Foucault, 1975). However, in this case, the job of the progressive discourse analyst is surely to publicize the analyses presented by these groups rather than expropriate them, rather than presenting them as if they were ours. To unravel the rhetorical tricks of those in power is part of politics, and you don't have to be a discourse analyst to do that.

24 The next problem is to do with normalization, and normalizing powers, of the discipline. Clearly, the rise of a particular approach within the academe is overdetermined, but there are certain dilemmas, not to mention dangers of ahistoricism at work here. There is something colonizing about the current vogue for discourse analysis which invites people retrospectively to recast what they have done as 'discourse analysis' or persuades us to 'recognize' them as 'really' being discourse analysts. The drive to constitute a specific method or area called 'discourse analysis' can be seen as arising from the pressures of academic practice. This stems from the need to discover new approaches, get jobs and establish corporate identities (such as 'discourse units') within a market-oriented academic landscape. There are many powerful studies of language around, and you don't have to be a discourse analyst to take them seriously.

In this last cluster of three problems, the connection with politics is clearly at issue. Now we want to turn explicitly to the politics of discourse analysis.

Discourse and politics

Is the progressive political impulse associated with discourse work a necessary or intrinsic feature of the approach? This is a vital question for researchers who turn to discourse-analytic research because it seems to offer a critical framework, not only for understanding accounts (the 'data') but also for understanding why the rest of psychology cannot deal with textual material. It is important to address this question in order to counter the general reformist and recuperative dynamic of academic practice (that is, the way the academic world absorbs criticisms and makes them a part of itself and all the stronger as a result). Given the undoubtedly helpful work conducted within the framework of discourse analysis, as the preceding chapters indicate, it is tempting to see this critical dynamic as somehow inherent within the approach itself, rather than as simply a feature of the way it is used. We need to take care to distinguish between the radical or politicizing 'applications' of discourse analysis and any radical claims made for the theory itself. It does sometimes seem that such politics as do underlie varieties of discourse approaches are either ambiguous or even, occasionally, hostile to critical work. We will identify four problems here, and then four traps (additional corresponding problems) that occur when a researcher tries to escape these problems. (Board game to follow!)

Four political problems

25 The first is the problem of relativism. Acknowledging readings as multiple and mutually coexistent can work to usefully problematize and disrupt dominant accounts. Meanings are tied to the time and space in which they are elaborated, hence claims to universal timeless truths made by social sciences such as psychology are thrown into question. This is fine when we want to criticize or disrupt accounts by indicating how there is no fixed interpretation. We may do this when we want to challenge the truth claims of dominant psychological models for example. However, it becomes difficult, using this model, to elaborate a position where it is possible to privilege or maintain a commitment to one reading rather than another (Burman, 1992b). In other words, a motivated, partisan political orientation is proscribed. Theory floats disconnected from any political position, and this is a return to a disturbingly familiar liberal pluralist position.

26 The problem of difference is connected to that of liberal pluralism in discourse analysis. The attention to variability, and then to difference within the discourse framework which initially seemed so fruitful and sympathetic to feminist concerns, for example, has proved to be limited in practice. There is a necessary conceptual link between notions of 'variability' in language and of 'difference' in meaning. The emphasis on the specificity of situations, and of socio-historical conditions tends towards a fragmentation of positions, making collective action

difficult. Such collective action would necessarily be 'unitary' (bring things together as one type of force or 'collective subject'), and would sit uncomfortably with discourse analysis's critique of the rational integrated subject (Eagleton, 1991).

27 The attention to difference then brings in its wake the 'problem' of resistance, or of making resistance problematic. The notion of discursive position has been a fruitful area for the politicized use of discourse analysis. Analysts have shown how it is possible to use multiple positionings within discourse to negotiate power relations (Hudson, 1984; Walkerdine, 1981). Yet where difference reigns supreme, so resistance threatens to be envisaged primarily only as residing within the individual. Although of all the theorists contributing to the discourse 'package', Foucault (1980, 1976/1981) has the most developed and explicit analysis of power, this is still located within individual and spontaneous reactions (capillaries of micro-power resisted by the body), rather than planned, directed struggle. Power is seen as so distributed within the mutual and changing relations of institutions as to remain an intangible and inescapable condition of subjectivity. The analysis of power as all-pervasive threatens to usher in an exhausted and passive fatalism and surrender of political vision. If power is everywhere, and where there is power there is resistance, then why bother trying to change the order of things?

28 The issue of reflexivity becomes a problem when it becomes part of the solution. Reflexivity has been useful in exploring researcher involvement and effects. However, focusing on the researcher's construction of the account rather than what is being accounted for has its problems too. Here, the key question concerns the status of the account. This issue crops up in the form of worries about how everything is being reduced to discourse, for how can we interpret anything if all meanings relate only to each other and not to something outside? Self-referentiality breeds solipsism. We agree with those who wish to focus on signification, language as productive when it has no 'referents' outside (Henriques *et al.*, 1998), but it is also important to hold onto some notion of representation. Representation and interpretation presuppose the independent existence of that which is represented or interpreted, but a strong discourse position tries to deny this. First, the emphasis can shift the focus to the account rather than what is being accounted for. Second, wallowing in the researcher's interpretive assumptions and processes can detract from the importance of the topic and possible political interventions. Third, agonizing about subjectivity and power can lead worried researchers to abandon the project of making interventions that go beyond reflexive concerns because of anxieties about exploitation or the paternalist relations set up in research.

Attempts to escape the problems: four more problems

In the attempts of researchers to grapple with the four problems we have just identified, there is a danger that the attention to subjectivity could work in four equally deleterious ways.

29 It can work to treat interpretive processes as matters to be confessed as interfering with the account (as when the research is said to be merely 'subjective').
30 It can work to constitute the account (as when the research is offered as one person's valid opinion of what is happening).
31 The subjectivity of interpretation could be seen as detaching the analysis from reality, rather than explicitly positioning the researcher within the research (as when the research is claimed to be 'just' an account).
32 If all research is rendered only fictive, then it can be said that we cannot make material interventions with our work, because our work is just another fiction. (This arises, for example, when the researcher claims that they had 'no effects' on their interviewees.)

Taking these problems together, we start to glimpse the vista of interpretive regress, and political immobilization, that could lie ahead for overenthusiastic discourse analysts. What this review of political problems with discourse analysis suggests is that it does not offer a political position in its own right: The politics can only lie in the strategic appropriation of the framework.

This, indeed, is the position that is developing among feminists who have been using discourse work (in its broadest sense) outside psychology. Discourse frameworks were taken up by feminists in particular as providing a welcome relief from single-factor models of oppression which deny or devalue varieties of struggle. However, the reception of discourse analysis by feminists has shifted from an initial enthusiasm (e.g. Weedon, 1987) to increasing caution emerging from across a spectrum of disciplines as diverse as philosophy (Lovibond, 1989), geography (Bondi, 1990), film theory (Creed, 1987; Penley, 1989) and cultural studies (Moore, 1988).

Conclusions and directions

This survey of thirty-two problems with discourse-analytic research is not exhaustive. There may be fifty-seven varieties of problem! Some points we have noted here have been developed at greater length elsewhere (Burman, 1991), and there have been other criticisms of discourse analysis outlined by different writers (Bowers, 1988; Abrams and Hogg, 1990). The problems we have identified have, in some cases, been problems to do with the turn to language in psychology, particularly in its post-structuralist forms (Burman, 1990).

Discourse analysis will undoubtedly develop in ways which will 'solve' some of the problems, and make others worse. Directions that the approach is moving in, or could move in, have been identified at meetings of discourse researchers. Figueroa and López (1991) noted five striking 'absences' in their encounter with discourse analysis in Britain, absences which we can here note also as suggestions for issues that discourse analysis could turn to address. Each absence also signifies something important about the state and future of discourse analysis: (i) the methodological process by which the material was produced (masked by an implicit intuitivism in some cases); (ii) discussion of the institutional appropriation of the 'method' as part of the apparatus of traditional psychology; (iii) the relation between discourse and modes of production, not only in texts studied but in the approach (why this approach now?); (iv) the link between the rise of discourse analysis and the contemporary 'crisis of knowledge' (postmodernity and the suchlike); and (v) how the analysis of discourse is related to the cultural space which is its context (for example, in the ideological and political forms of British society).

These absences, and perhaps we could take them now alongside the thirty-two problems, raise all the traditional questions of models and morals of research in psychology, and more. The positions outlined in the chapters in this book do offer visions for making worthwhile political interventions using discourse analysis. This activity may take a variety of forms. Discourse analysts now can champion the cause of a particular discourse by elaborating the contrasting consequences of each discursive framework, and can promote an existing (perhaps subordinate) discourse (as the 'empowerment', 'giving people a voice' model of research). We can intervene directly in clarifying consequences of discursive frameworks with speakers (as in training or action research, for example), as well as commenting on the discursive-political consequences of discursive clashes and frameworks. If we do not do one or all of these, we will be assimilated into mainstream empiricist research. We would then find our work relayed among the repertoires of the discipline, rather than offering, as it should, critical readings of its texts.

6 Discourse analysis and micronations of the self in times of war

This final chapter takes forward the argument about the problem of recuperation and psychologization of discourse analysis, and provides a worked example of different forms of discourse analysis undertaken in political and social contexts outside psychology. I am also concerned here with the way that discourse analysis functions as a specialist approach in psychology that overlooks how people outside the discipline always carry out a form of discourse analysis that is critical of the texts they read. A number of different oppositional cultural and political movements have carried out their own critiques of the dominant ideology that are actually more interesting than our academic discourse analysis.

The chapter outlines problems with contemporary discourse analysis – a focus on everyday conversation, interpersonal interaction, formal sequences, correct explication and disciplinary segregation – problems that replicate general problems with the discipline of psychology (the gaze upon those outside its domain, reduction to the level of the individual, abstraction of behaviour and cognitive processes, claims to interpretative authority and avoidance of politics as such).

Approaches to discursive practice are described from within one of the recently formed 'micronations', NSK, which also provide a new way of thinking about the role of psychology in broader social processes (that is, of the impact of psychologization). Alternative principles for discursive practice are derived from this description: turning the gaze back onto psychology and the ideological forces that give rise to it; treating forms of representation as sites

> for the relay of power; tracing how social forms are treated as contextually and historically situated; highlighting forms of discursive practice that open up spaces for interpretation and argument about the nature of interpretation; and connecting contradictory individual affective forces with the realm of political struggle.

The Queen of England is reported to have confided to a butler, of the mysteries surrounding the death of Diana, Princess of Wales, that 'There are dark forces at work, of which we know nothing' (Blackburn, 2005: xv–xvi). This comment would not be out of place in medieval times, and then there would be a fairly clear demarcation between the forces of good and evil. Those would be understood to be external forces which then might tempt and recruit individuals. Under capitalism, however, there is a shift of focus so that at the same time that there is still a belief in dark conspiracies of which we know nothing, or next to nothing; there is also a search for dark forces of which we know nothing, or next to nothing, inside individuals. The notion that we know next to nothing about these dark forces brings us to an edge of knowledge and reason, and it comes to define human psychology as a site of investigation which contains mysteries.

The Queen's reference to 'dark forces' also draws attention to the enduring concern with purity of a nation state which is threatened by black darkness and confusion, and which conjures up in the Western imagination the chaotic savage world outside Europe, perhaps even in this case just outside English territory (Achcar, 2006). With the arrival of capitalism the metaphoric structure of the civilized community is separated into twin aspects. The nation and the self complement one another such that the nation is conceived as a body politic and the self comes to be guarded as if it were a microscopic nation. Then the discipline of psychology comes to operate like a state apparatus, defining and regulating good conduct and allegiance to bodily forms treated as homologous to geographical territory. It is the disavowed connection between nation and self, and between discipline and state, that gives ideological weight to the subject of psychology, both individual and disciplinary subject (Parker, 2007b).

At a time of neoliberal deregulation of welfare services and intensified individualization, also a time of state surveillance and the concentration of power in the old imperialist centres, it is indeed as if we are in a war governed by forces that we know next to nothing about. There are at least three levels to this war, and they are intertwined. There is a first level of war over geographical territory which does often proceed in a virtually mediated way – both for combatants and a global audience – that it does, at the same time, make sense to say that the war does and does not actually take place (Baudrillard, 1995). There is a second level of war, of collusion in the war by psychologists in which the war of terror pulls the American Psychological Association, for example, into legitimizing the use of torture on those who are thereby rendered into a kind of non-human 'bare life' (Agamben, 1998). And there is a third level of war, one that seems trivial in comparison with the first two levels, but which is still, for many of those fighting for a certain kind of rationality in academic and clinical research, a war over scientific paradigms inside psychology; it is as if each side insists to the other that 'you are not to win this war, you cannot win this war' (Parker, 2007b).

Discourse analysis

This brings me to the apparently most trivial dispute in psychology, over the role of discourse analysis. Discourse analysis in the discipline of psychology was, from the start, a contest over language and definitions of language. It seemed at one point as if the stakes of the argument over discourse in psychology were over the very existence of psychology as a separate discipline (Parker, 2002, 2004). My argument now is that those of us who made a turn to discourse in psychology made a necessary mistake – that is, we argued on grounds that we could not choose – but now it is necessary to recognize that we cannot win this war on these grounds. We must find a different place for discourse analysis that connects with political practice. If we do not do that, then discourse analysis will have no positive role in some of the new debates about 'critical psychology' that are appearing inside the discipline.

I do not intend to dwell on critical psychology now, for my task is instead to address the question of discourse analysis in the discipline. However, we should briefly remind ourselves about some key characteristics of the discipline that we all face, and I am concerned here with the type of mainstream Anglo-American psychology which is currently hegemonic: it rarely includes itself in the phenomena it studies, keeping its gaze directed at those outside the discipline who are assumed to be non-psychologists who are routinely deceived and misrepresented; it reduces phenomena to the level of the individual, and this reduction proceeds both downwards from the level of social processes and upwards from the level of physiological functions; it reproduces an abstracted model of behavioural sequences and cognitive mechanisms in which each individual is assumed to operate as a miniature version of the operational forms that define positivist investigation; it often pretends to merely describe human activity, but this description requires a degree of declared or surreptitious interpretation that prescribes a correct version of events; and it subscribes to a form of objectivity, fake neutrality which obscures the enduring role of personal, institutional and political stakes in the formulation of research questions (Parker, 2007a).

It is not necessary to call oneself a critical psychologist to argue for an approach that aims to address the problems that we face in mainstream psychology by asking the following questions: How is 'psychology' produced as a commonsensical resource for individuals to make sense of themselves and others and of possibilities for changing social conditions? How are social processes reproduced and maintained at the level of interpersonal interaction and individual experience, at the level of 'psychology'? How are patterns of activity structured to replicate power relations regardless of and even despite the immediate intentions of an individual 'psychology'? How can theoretical articulation of the place of individual 'psychology' and social structure be developed to provide some critical distance from ideology? How can research into the political functions of 'psychology' operate in such a way as to maintain a degree of autonomy of activity and experience from political interference (Parker, 2007b)? There have been many working in discourse analysis, and I include here those working in conversation analysis, discursive psychology and Foucauldian analysis, who have addressed these questions. That questioning is a function of the marginal, even 'critical', position of discourse analysts in the early years.

However, here I want to highlight the problems that bedevil discourse analysis as it comes to be an accepted part of the discipline, a process that turns the approach into a further obstacle to critical research in addition to the other problems of psychology I identified so far. It should be clearer then why the turn to discourse was a mistake (if a necessary mistake), and why we now need to strike out on another path. I include myself in this mistake, and you might take this as the moment when I recant and tell you why you should not now take the route I once took to get here (Parker, 1992a, 2002). I will highlight five problems with discourse analysis, suggest some alternative principles for radical research into discursive practice and illustrate this with a little piece of text which I will unravel and contextualize along the way.

Darkness

Let us begin with the text, first as a bare text. As I re-present it to you now you will immediately notice, if you have been schooled in the conversation analysis tradition of discourse analysis, that I have not marked every pause, intake of breath and its articulation with the sounds around it (Potter, 1998). This version was recorded in 1986, and released to the public in 1987. The peculiar shape of the text already raises some intriguing questions about transcription which conversation analysis could help us with here, but we will sidestep these questions to stay focused on broader issues about the nature of discourse and how we might work with it. In its 1986 context, this block of lines is repeated three times.

> You are in black darkness and confusion.
> You have been hugger-muggered and carom-shotted into a war,
> and you know nothing about it.
> You know nothing about the forces that caused it,
> or you know next to nothing.
> You are not to win this war.
> You cannot win this war.

There are already some evident peculiarities of the text, particularly as it was intended for as large an audience as possible, and two mysterious hyphenated words, 'hugger-muggered' and 'carom-shotted' could be read as reiterating the overt message that there are forces of which 'you know nothing' or 'you know next to nothing'. The 'black darkness and confusion' of the first line are evoked in the second line so that, in classic semiological terms, the first line 'denotes' a physical and experiential state – your 'black darkness and confusion' – and the second line 'connotes' it to replicate the sense that 'you know nothing' about the forces of language even as you know something – that is 'next to nothing' rather than nothing as such – in order for the lines to appear to make sense.

A standard dictionary helps with 'hugger-muggered', and it tells us that this is a synthesis of fifteenth and sixteenth century English terms for 'huddle' and 'conceal'. So, as the past participle of a verb, you have also been 'hugger-muggered' into a conspiratorial worldview by these lines. The word 'carom-shotted' is more obscure; the 'carom' is possibly derived from the Spanish for cannon, *carambola*, which is sometimes used figuratively to describe a trick or a ruse. In billiards a 'carom-shot' describes how one ball can be cannoned against another in order to drive it in a certain direction. So, here in these lines we have a clever replication of the indirectness of cause; we are cannoned into a war by something that is not the first cause, and so we can only know 'next to nothing' about 'the forces that caused it'. It could not then be possible to win a war which is structured in such a way that its causes can be evoked but not fully known.

This first approach to the bare text is closer to a literary-critical reading than what often passes for discourse analysis in psychology today, but it is necessary to tackle some of the rhetorical, even poetic, devices that give sense to the lines. We will need to go well beyond standard discourse analysis to unravel and contextualize this text, and we will thereby learn some lessons about shortcomings of and alternatives to discourse analysis as we proceed. So, let me turn now to five problems with dominant approaches to language-use in the discipline (Parker, 2012).

Everyday conversation

There is an increasing tendency to focus on everyday conversation. A false opposition is often set up between interviews on the one hand and 'naturally occurring' conversation on the other to warrant research on what is then supposed to be ordinary talk (e.g. Edwards and Potter, 1992). In a research interview we still, at least, have the option of attending to how the psychologist structures the interaction (and there have been some very good conversation analysis studies devoted to this structuring), including them in the phenomenon being studied. The focus on everyday conversation, in contrast, is complicit with the gaze of mainstream psychology on the activity of others supposed to be non-psychologists.

Instead, we need to (i) focus on the use made of psychology in the public domain, and (ii) focus on the reproduction of the conditions in which psychological explanations come to assume importance. That is, we need to reflexively question dominant forms of knowledge and our own inclusion in those dominant forms.

The text about 'black darkness and confusion' serves as a nice example about such an inclusion of positions of reading, writing and interpretation, and there are specific reasons for this that can then guide us in thinking about what discourse does and what we could do with it. The text comes from the track 'F.I.A.T.' on an album called *Opus Dei* (Monroe, 2005). I am unravelling this bit by bit so we can appreciate some of the layers of meaning that are at work here. The simple frame of the title, 'F.I.A.T.' is enigmatic, which is in keeping with the sense that 'you know nothing about the forces that caused it', or you know next to nothing', and while lyrics of other tracks are given on the album cover of *Opus Dei*, these lyrics are not. That it may be a reference to the automobile manufacturer FIAT seems to be dispelled when we go up a frame to the album title, for if 'Opus Dei' means 'God's Work' then it would make more sense for us to remove the punctuation marks and run the letters together to give 'Fiat' as 'Let it be' as in God's words 'Fiat Lux', 'Let it be light', or, here as well, 'Let there be light' in the 'black darkness and confusion'.

The album title also connotes confusion and conspiracy, for the organization 'Opus Dei' is known to be a secretive organization inside the Catholic Church which is also implicated in fascist politics. That brings us to the band responsible for this album, a band which is also often accused of being fascist. It is Laibach, whose name was itself a provocation when it was formed in 1980 in Trbovlie in Slovenia, which was at that time the northernmost nation of the Socialist Federal Republic of Yugoslavia. The capital of Slovenia is Ljubljana, and so to adopt the German name 'Laibach' was enough to get the band banned. Laibach became an integral part of a constellation of cultural-political forces called 'New Slovenian Art' commonly referred to using the German designation *Neue Slowenische Kunst* or 'NSK'. It is possible for these purposes to refer to Laibach and NSK interchangeably, and other components of NSK do the artwork for Laibach album covers and publicity (Arns, 2003).

One of the interesting things about NSK is that there is embedded in its explicit critique of 'dissidence' as a strategy in Eastern Europe also an implicit critique of everyday psychology. The NSK *Laibach Kunst* manifesto set itself against the Slovenian alternative movements and in particular against the claim that 'dissidence' could operate as a personal space in which the dissident thinks they can thereby be free of the state and party apparatus. The argument was that this personal space was actually a prerequisite for the regime to function, and the level of psychology as ideally separable from political context served as a buffer zone in which people could complain, feel free and tolerate the bureaucracy. The *Laibach Kunst* manifesto called instead for 'the principle of conscious rejection of personal tastes, judgements, convictions' and for 'free depersonalisation, voluntary acceptance of the role of ideology'. To be in 'black darkness and confusion' while listening to the album *Opus Dei* is therefore to embrace obscure forces instead of attempting to master them, and any pretence to bring light is itself seen as an ideological ruse (Čufer and Irwin, 1992).

The role of the 'everyday' as seeming to be free of structuring forces is thus thrown into question, and we have, instead, attention directed to the way certain forms of discursive practice produce and reproduce forms of psychology. Against discourse analysis that focuses on everyday conversation, then, we turn the gaze back onto psychology and the ideological forces that give rise to it. This first principle needs to be interlinked with other arguments, so let us move on to another problem with discourse analysis.

Interpersonal interaction

There is a focus nowadays on interpersonal interaction. Even though there is often an explicit attention to the interaction as such rather than a search for cognitive processes inside the heads of participating individuals, this focus on interpersonal interaction is still at the expense of analysis of broader power relations (e.g. Edwards, 1992). Rare attempts to embed interpersonal interaction in systems of patriarchal authority, for example, then also necessarily have to break from psychology and from the forms of discourse analysis tolerated by psychology. The focus on interpersonal interaction is actually of a piece with the broader project of psychology, which is to reduce description and explanation to small-scale interaction, if possible to the mental operations of the individuals involved.

Instead (and with the point numbering here following the sequence begun in the last section), we need to (iii) show how power relations are reiterated in the interpersonal realm and (iv) show how ostensibly individual processes are mobilized by wider networks of power. That is, we question notions of motivation or stake as explanatory devices, turning instead to how performances maintain the positions of those who speak, listen and interpret.

Here, the cultural-political interventions of NSK provide an example of how to work with discourse in such a way as to avoid reduction to a psychological or even an interpersonal level of explanation. The circuit of irrational appeals to irrational authority – 'Fiat' embedded in 'Opus Dei' – and the refusal of any supposition of an enlightened rational authority that would explain away 'forces' that lead to 'confusion' circumvent any knowing author, even any knowing author who will tell those who hear the message that this is a game. The refusal to drop the mask thus keeps this mystifying circuit going so that while we might suspect that this is a performance of some kind, Laibach will not tell us what it is a performance of, except of the sense that we 'know nothing' or 'next to nothing'.

A disturbing aspect of Laibach's performances through the 1980s, when this text was released, and the 1990s after the Yugoslav state had disintegrated, was that the band always appeared in public in uniform. Members of the band never dropped the mask in order to reassure their audience that they merely appeared to be fascist but were not really so (Žižek, 1993a). This kind of performance thus disrupted the attempt to anchor and explain the performance by way of individual intention, and instead there was a short circuit between the level of the performance, when the band told the audience they were in 'black darkness and confusion', and the highest levels of the Yugoslav state, whose authority they replicated and so undermined. The message that 'you cannot win this war' was released as conflicts between different national groups in the Yugoslav state were starting to turn to violence; this is the year Slobodan Milošević visited Kosovo and declared his support for Serb nationalist aspirations there (Magaš, 1993; Jeffs, 1995).

Inside Slovenia, this year, 1987, was when the 'poster scandal' erupted and ended Yugoslav Youth Day, which was also not coincidentally Tito's birthday. A poster submitted by the NSK New Collectivism design group won the competition for best poster, but after the panel of judges had declared that the winning design embodied the spirit of Yugoslav socialist youth, it was revealed it was based on a 1936 Nazi propaganda poster (Stepančič, 1994). So, rather than opt for 'dissidence', the NSK had embraced the ideology, and embraced it so effectively that it was dismantled from within. No appeal to what the authors really meant was necessary, and instead the forms of representation and their function in historically constituted symbolic regimes of power were turned against themselves.

Here, the level of the 'interpersonal' is not privileged over other levels of practice, and a reduction to the level of individual mental processes is neatly sidestepped. Against discourse analysis that keeps focused on interpersonal interaction, then, we have a way of working with discursive practice that connects with the level of individual judgement in such a way as to question it. Forms of representation are treated as sites for the relay of power, and so there is a quite different way of locating the place of interventions that interpret and maintain or change social conditions. This is the second principle of an alternative approach to discursive practice. Let us move on to see how we can arrive at a third.

Formal sequences

There is a focus in discourse analysis now on formal sequences of interaction. These formal sequences proceed regardless of any particular content, and this also means that meaningful context is usually wiped out of the analysis as part of an attempt to avoid an appeal to the real meaning intended by social actors (e.g. Antaki, 2008). This is also the rationale for avoiding ethical complications that might arise if interpretations are given to participants who may disagree with what is said by the discourse analyst about what they have said. This focus on form at the expense of content repeats the endeavour of so-called scientific psychology to replace meaning given to situations by people with mechanistic and often dehumanizing re-descriptions of their behaviour and hidden cognitive mechanisms.

Instead, we need to (v) show how formal devices are injected with particular content and (vi) show how formal devices are resignified in different social contexts. In this way, we show how symbolic forms operate as part of a historical process, and how formal devices carry the weight of history, repeating and transforming social conditions.

The tearing of political images from context was one of the characteristics of punk in the West, and the appearance of punk in Slovenia kick-started the opposition movement in the late 1970s. Strategies of *détournement* used by the situationists were also influential, and were also employed by NSK (Spanke, 2003). In the naming of the 'F.I.A.T.' track, for example, there is an anticipation of the Laibach album released a year later in which there is replication and resignification of the Beatles album *Let It Be* (Monroe, 2005). On the Laibach version of 'Let it be' every track from the original album is re-presented, except the cover track 'Let it be'. So, for example, the first track 'Get back' includes the original lyrics 'Get back to where you once belonged' but intoned with some menace by men in uniform the latent fascist implications are brought to the surface. Similarly, on *Opus Dei*, the Queen track 'One vision' includes the original lyrics calling for an ecstatic celebration of 'one nation', but now in German on the Laibach track 'Geburt Einer Nation' (a title which also resonates with the proto-fascist film *Birth of the Nation* which in 1915 celebrated the formation of the Ku Klux Klan in the United States).

There is another crucially important process of resignification at work in the track 'F.I.A.T.', one that now comes to light if some of those peculiar phrases are typed into internet search engines. It transpires that there is a connection between the initial letters that spell out 'Let it be' and the car industry, in FIAT operating in Italy next-door to Slovenia, a former occupying power under Mussolini, and there are some outstanding historical territorial claims made by nationalists on both the Italian and Slovene side. The block of lines is resignified in one period of upheaval and impending war in 1980s Yugoslavia from Italy in 1942, for it is in that year, on 13 July, that these words were first composed and broadcast from Radio Rome to the US American forces entering the war in Europe.

The radio broadcast is 'Darkness' by Ezra Pound, and so the message to the Americans is that they have been 'hugger-muggered and carom-shotted into a war' and that they 'know nothing about the forces that caused it' or 'next to nothing' (Tiffany, 1990). The re-placing of the lines in their original context has the effect of filling them with a different meaning, but while this does appear to provide an explanation of the rather archaic and bizarre tenor of the text now, this resignification also then throws into question the intentional authorship of the lines replicated as a track on a Laibach album.

NSK provide their own theoretical gloss on this activity of resignification in which a 'retroactive' principle in the production of art is anchored by the use of apparently purely formal devices. One of their key reference points is the abstract art movement 'Suprematism' founded by Kazimir Malevich in Russia before the Revolution, and which was recruited as an avant-garde agitprop resource in the creative ferment during the early years of the Soviet Union (Mudrak, 2001). Known for the 'Black Circle, and a 'Black Square' and 'Black Cross' that appear over and over again in NSK art projects and as symbolic material on Laibach's uniforms, Malevich himself is resignified. These are perfect motifs to evoke 'black darkness and confusion'. Malevich was never a Bolshevik, but re-presented as if he was one, not even a Russian but now claimed by the Ukraine, and NSK draw on these external resources along with other elements of Soviet socialist realist and German national socialist iconography to construct an authentic Slovenian Art (Gržnic, 2004).

Here there is a turn by NSK to formal properties of representation, but precisely in order to disrupt the reduction to form as such. Against discourse analysis which either attempts to reduce meaningful activity to formal sequences, and against phenomenological alternatives that privilege content as a reaction against such a reduction to form, we can see how discursive practices constitute and reconstitute symbolic forms. So, we have a third principle elaborated now in a quite different approach to discourse in which we trace how social forms are treated as contextually and historically situated mobilizing contradictory competing ideological contents. Let us move on to a fourth problem with discourse analysis in psychology.

Correct explication

There is a focus on the correct explication of talk. Despite the repeated invocation of ethnomethodological principles concerning members' own sense-making, conversation analysis proceeds by way of a detailed re-description of talk using a specialist vocabulary that translates a complicated transcription of interaction (e.g. Atkinson and Heritage, 1984). Other forms of discourse analysis that aim to discover 'discourses' or 'repertoires' proceed in much the same way, replacing the actual text with a theoretical redescription which also functions as an interpretation. This is very much in keeping with psychology's reinterpretation of behaviour in terms of cognitive mechanisms or paraphernalia in some other particular vocabulary.

Instead, we need to (vii) learn from the way actually existing interpretations and reinterpretations contest versions of reality and (viii) attend to contested spaces in which there is struggle over the nature of correct explication. This means working with antagonistic and open forms of discursive practice that question any closed consensual ideological systems of meaning.

So, we can see in the case of NSK that 'voluntary acceptance of the role of ideology' is a strategy of immersion in discourse that avoids the ideological trap of imagining that we can comment on discourse from a position that is completely independent of it. For NSK, it is the idea that one can speak outside ideological systems that underpinned the 'dissident' position in Eastern Europe, and this idea of a personal free space is also one that consoles consumers and audiences of political propaganda in the capitalist world. And, the position from which one is spoken to about forces of which we know 'next to nothing' is not attributed with any more superior knowledge than we have ourselves (Žižek, 1994).

My NSK informants tell me that the message from Ezra Pound's 'Darkness' broadcast was directed not only to Pound, who was caught in the 'black darkness and confusion' of Italian fascism and then madness after his capture by the Americans. It was a message that was also directed at themselves, NSK, a reminder that the artist has no necessarily privileged position to comment on the political matters they intervene in.

Nationality and statehood provide anchors for the self, and they mimic and reproduce the ideological claim that there is an authentic 'identity' that can be pitted against outside forces. A seemingly independent Slovene state was the first nation to be levered out of the Yugoslav federation by the West in 1991, and NSK, who had been assembling its own version of authentic Slovene identity quite deliberately assembled from outside the nation, responded by setting up its own state, NSK State in Time. The NSK embassy in Sarajevo in 1995 distributed diplomatic passports that were so convincing that some people were able to get out of Bosnia-Herzegovina during the civil war. Laibach, which played in Sarajevo as part of its 'Occupied Europe Tour', play a specific role in the NSK State in Time as the politicians. There are state artists (the Irwin group) and a state church (Cosmokinetic Theatre Noordung), and together with the New Collectivism design group, this cluster of cultural-political organizations provides through their own state apparatus citizenship to everyone who applies, regardless of geographical territory (Arns, 1998).

This state is a State in Time, not in any particular territory, and so it dismantles our assumptions about allegiance to an identity that is organized around a centre, the kind of identity valued under capitalism. There is therefore also a dismantling of the state apparatus of the self that is the discipline of psychology. It should also be noted that the NSK State in Time is not democratic and does not pretend to be an open consensual space in which all citizens participate freely. There are ongoing projects to accumulate the historical experiences of those with NSK passports, and the Irwin group is currently working with accounts by Nigerian NSK passport holders. But, the passport offices, for example, are deliberately structured so as to replicate the state apparatus and to repeat and thereby question the authoritarian nature of all forms of state and identity (Žižek, 1993b).

Insistence on the antagonistic, non-consensual character of discourse throws into question the supposed independence of academic researchers and their comfortable assumption that they are in a position to explain what other people mean. Against discourse analysis that pretends to provide a correct explication, then, we highlight forms of discursive practice that open up spaces for interpretation and argument about the nature of interpretation.

Disciplinary segregation

We now turn to the fifth problem with discourse analysis, which is that there is a studious avoidance of politics. This avoidance ranges from the claim that a researcher should not talk about power in their analysis of a text if the issue of power is not actually topicalized there, to the rhetorical strategy of warding off political questions by insisting that these are not part of the research and might be dealt with in another academic department (e.g. Hepburn and Wiggins, 2007). This sub-disciplinary specialization in discourse which seals off that domain of work from other areas of work fits all too neatly in the confines of disciplinary segregation that psychologists want to keep in place, and it is the ground for the pretend 'neutrality' of psychological research.

Instead, we need to (ix) show how politics frames psychological work and (x) show the ways in which the process of psychologization in contemporary society is profoundly political. This means connecting apparently individual affective responses to symbolic material with political processes.

This raises particular questions here about the appeal of the 'F.I.A.T.' text and the way a form of reader response is constructed that resonates with ambiguities and uncertainties at the political level. We have noted how the use of particular turns of phrase – 'hugger-muggered and carom-shotted' – evokes, as part of the texture of the message, the 'confusion' it describes. The peculiar formulation that 'you know next to nothing' about the forces that caused this war has a sinister edge to it because it elicits the sense that we as individuals have intimations of what we know which may be true but which we cannot trust, and the sense that there are political forces that cause us to do things that we have confused and incomplete suspicions about.

It is not surprising that a fascist broadcast should hint at conspiracies, but Pound's craft at rhetoric connects global conspiracy with the sense that each alienated individual has that they do not fully know what lies within themselves. A version of individual psychology is thus part of the political force of the Pound broadcast, and it is then embedded in another political frame by Laibach. As a counterpart to the Pound broadcast, the album *Opus Dei* includes another later track 'The great seal' which is a pompous slow march with words by Winston Churchill, the speech declaring that 'we will fight them on the beaches' (Monroe, 2005).

The music and lyrics are reworked on Laibach's 2006 album *Volk* as the national anthem of NSK, and has the added words 'we will fight to defend our state'. The *Volk* album comprises détourned national anthems, some with very little changes to the original lyrics but resignified through the use of different beats to the music and now, in some cases, with images in accompanying videos. The 'Anglia' track, for example has taunting verse references to the English imagining they are still ruling the world, that 'all nations are inferior, any sedition hushed, rebellious Scots crushed'. The references to crushing the Scots are actually still there in a rarely sung fourth verse of the real English national anthem, and on the Laibach version the chorus concludes with 'God save your gracious Queen, God save you all.' The video has the figure of an elderly lady dressed in robes force-feeding an English cooked breakfast to manacled prisoners. Videos accompanying some of the anthems can be found on the Laibach section of the nskstate.com website and, of course, on YouTube. A post-9/11 US tour was called 'Divided States of America', under the publicity slogan 'United we Fall'.

Political symbols are thus deployed by NSK to bring to the surface the always already present political resonances and functions of discourse. As the Yugoslav state disintegrated at the end of the 1980s and tried to extract itself from the civil war that was engulfing Croatia, Serbia and Bosnia-Herzegovina, NSK intervened in a quite deliberate way to heighten the tension. Street posters were posted by the NSK New Collectivism group, the group that had been behind the 'poster scandal' in 1987, and the posters made explicit an assumption in Slovenia that the Western free-market would solve their problems. One poster declared 'Buy victory!' Another poster, with words that were actually in Croatian instead of Slovene, went up on the streets of Ljubljana with the slogan 'I want to fight for a new Europe!' (Monroe, 2005). The role of politics in everyday life is thus brought into the open, and there is a refusal to segregate politics, to treat it as something that only politicians are concerned with or as something that concerns 'forces' of which we 'know nothing' or 'next to nothing'.

Against discourse analysis that tries to study language and the self without reference to wider social and historical context, and that plays the same game as psychology which shuts out political questions, we have a fifth principle for discursive practice being enacted by NSK, which is that we need to connect the realm of contradictory individual affective forces with the realm of political struggle.

Conclusions

It would be tempting, particular in light of the title of the 'F.I.A.T.' track, to say that we should turn to something that could be called 'auto-discourse-analytic' research, but this would risk making NSK discursive practice seem to be something spontaneous. Discourse analysts in psychology developed their work from quite specific theoretical frameworks, even if they sometimes now pretend that they are simply doing good empirical research, and the kinds of discourse analysis I have described are also embedded in complex theoretical traditions of work. And we have to also draw the lesson that our relation to existing theoretically informed discursive practice may now have to be quite different from that of academic researchers who pretend to find things out that other people did not already know. This critique of discourse analysis entails questions about what our role as allies, supporters and voices for actually existing discourse analysis outside the discipline should be. When we read a text about war from 1942 that is resignified in 1986 we are also faced with some questions about what the consequences might be of resignifying this text again in Europe edged by war.

NSK is one of many 'micronations' today that playfully subvert the claims of nation states to define and maintain the individual identities of their subjects. Some of these micronations are formed by individuals carving out their own territory or are set up by charitable organizations that explicitly raise questions about international citizenship in times of mass migration (Fussell, 2004). NSK and NSK State in Time, however, raise the political stakes to create antagonistic discursive spaces, resignifying existing ideological forms to show how power relations are reiterated at every level of the social and so contest the conditions that make disciplinary apparatuses like psychology and forms of modern subjectivity possible (Parker, 2005b, 2007b, 2008). It shows an alternative way of working with discursive practice which is also, necessarily against discourse analysis in psychology today.

References

Abrams, D. and Hogg, M. (1990) 'The context of discourse: Let's not throw out the baby with the bathwater', *Philosophical Psychology*, 3(2), 219–225.

Achcar, G. (2006) *The Clash of Barbarisms: The Making of the New World Disorder*. London: Saqi Books.

Agamben, G. (1998) *Homo Sacer: Sovereign Power and Bare Life*. Stanford, CA: Stanford University Press.

Alldred, P. and Burman, E. (2005) 'Analysing children's accounts using discourse analysis', in S. Greene and D. Hogan (eds) *Researching Children's Experience: Approaches and Methods*. London: Sage.

Althusser, L. (1970/1971) 'Ideology and ideological state apparatuses (notes towards an investigation)', in L. Althusser, *Lenin and Philosophy, and Other Essays*. London: New Left Books.

Althusser, L. (1971) *Lenin and Philosophy, and Other Essays*. London: New Left Books.

Amundson, J. (1994) 'Whither narrative? The danger of getting it right', *Journal of Marital and Family Therapy*, 20(1), 83–87.

Andersen, R. (1988) *The Power and the Word: Language, Power and Change*. London: Paladin.

Anderson, H. and Goolishian, H. (1992) 'The client is the expert: A not-knowing approach to therapy', in S. McNamee and K.J. Gergen (eds) *Therapy as Social Construction*. London: Sage.

Antaki, C. (2008) 'Formulations in psychotherapy', in A. Peräkylä, C. Antaki, S. Vehviläinen and I. Leudar (eds) *Conversation Analysis of Psychotherapy*. Cambridge: Cambridge University Press.

Archard, D. (1984) *Consciousness and the Unconscious*. London: Hutchinson.

Armistead, N. (ed.) (1974) *Reconstructing Social Psychology*. Harmondsworth: Penguin.

Arns, I. (1998) 'Mobile states/shifting borders/moving entities: The Slovenian artist's collective Neue Slowenische Kunst (NSK)', in I. Arns (ed.) (2003) *IRWIN-RETROPRINCIP: 1983–2003*. Frankfurt: Revolver.

Arns, I. (ed.) (2003) *IRWINRETROPRINCIP: 1983–2003*. Frankfurt: Revolver.

Arribas-Ayllon, M. and Walkerdine, V. (2008) 'Foucauldian discourse analysis', in C. Willig and W. Stainton-Rogers (eds) *Handbook of Qualitative Research in Psychology*. London: Sage.

References

Atkinson, J. and Heritage, J. (eds) (1984) *Structures of Social Action: Studies in Conversation Analysis*. Cambridge: Cambridge University Press.

Austin, J.L. (1962) *How to Do Things with Words*. Oxford: Clarendon Press.

Badiou, A. (2005) *Being and Event*. New York: Continuum.

Banister, P., Bunn, G., Burman, E., Daniels, J., Duckett, P., Goodley, D., Lawthom, R., Parker, I., Runswick-Cole, K., Sixsmith, J., Smailes, S., Tindall, C. and Whelan, P. (2011) *Qualitative Methods in Psychology: A Research Guide* (revised second edition). Buckingham: Open University Press

Banister, P., Burman, E., Parker, I., Taylor, M. and Tindall, C. (1994) *Qualitative Methods in Psychology: A Research Guide*. Buckingham: Open University Press.

Barthes, R. (1967) 'The death of the author', in R. Barthes (1977) *Image – Music – Text*, London: Fontana.

Baudrillard, J. (1995) *The Gulf War Did Not Take Place*. Bloomington, IN: Indiana University Press.

Benjamin, W. (1939) 'Theses on the philosophy of history', in W. Benjamin (1973) *Illuminations*. London: Fontana.

Berger, P.L. (1965) 'Towards a sociological understanding of psychoanalysis', *Social Research*, 32(1), 26–41.

Bettelheim, B. (1986) *Freud and Man's Soul*. Harmondsworth: Peregrine.

Bhaskar, R. (1986) *Scientific Realism and Human Emancipation*. London: Verso.

Billig, M. (1976) *Social Psychology and Intergroup Relations*. London: Academic Press.

Billig, M. (1987) *Arguing and Thinking: A Rhetorical Approach to Social Psychology*. Cambridge: Cambridge University Press.

Billig, M. (1988) 'Methodology and scholarship in understanding ideological explanation', in I. Parker (ed.) (2011) *Critical Psychology: Critical Concepts in Psychology, Volume 2, Dominant Models of Psychology and Their Limits*. Abingdon/New York: Routledge.

Billig, M. (1991) *Ideology and Opinions: Studies in Rhetorical Psychology*. London: Sage.

Billig, M. (1993) 'Nationalism and Richard Rorty: The text as a flag for *Pax Americana*', *New Left Review*, 202, 69–83.

Billig, M., Condor, S., Edwards, D., Gane, M., Middleton, D. and Radley, A. (1988) *Ideological Dilemmas: A Social Psychology of Everyday Thinking*. London: Sage.

Blackburn, S. (2005) *Truth: A Guide for the Perplexed*. Harmondsworth: Penguin.

Blissett, L. (1997) 'Chew on this: Chewing gum and the rise of Glop Art', in S. Home (ed.) *Mind Invaders: A Reader in Psychic Warfare, Cultural Sabotage and Semiotic Terrorism*. London: Serpent's Tail.

BNAP (British Network for Alternatives to Psychiatry) (1988) 'Community Treatment Orders 2: Letter to Mental Health Commission', *Asylum: A Magazine for Democratic Psychiatry*, 12(3), 4–5.

Bocock, R. (1976) *Freud and Modern Society*. London: Van Nostrand Reinhold.

Bondi, L. (1990) 'Feminism, postmodernism and geography: Space for women? Feminism and postmodernism', *Antipode*, 22(2), 15–67.

Bowers, J. (1988) 'Essay review of *Discourse and Social Psychology*', *British Journal of Social Psychology*, 27(2), 185–192.

Bowers, J. and Iwi, K. (1991) 'Constructing society beyond discursive idealism and social constructionism', paper for Second Discourse Analysis Workshop/Conference, Manchester Polytechnic, July.

Braun, V. and Clarke, V. (2006) 'Using thematic analysis in psychology', *Qualitative Research in Psychology*, 3(2), 77–101.

Brown, S. and Stenner, P. (2009) *Psychology Without Foundations: History, Philosophy and Psychological Theory*. London: Sage.

Burman, E. (1990) 'Differing with deconstruction: A feminist critique', in I. Parker and J. Shotter (eds) *Deconstructing Social Psychology*. London: Routledge.

Burman, E. (1991) 'What discourse is not', *Philosophical Psychology*, 4(3), 325–342.

Burman, E. (1992a) 'Feminism and discourse in developmental psychology: Power, subjectivity and interpretation', *Feminism & Psychology*, 2(1), 45–59.

Burman, E. (1992b) 'Developmental psychology and the post-modern child', in J. Doherty, E. Graham and M. Malek (eds) *Postmodernism and the Social Sciences*, London: Macmillan.

Burman, E. (1992c) 'Identification and power in feminist therapy: A reflexive history of a discourse analysis', *Women's Studies International Forum*, 15(4), 487–498.

Burman, E. (1994) *Deconstructing Developmental Psychology*. London: Routledge.

Burman, E. (2008a) *Deconstructing Developmental Psychology* (second edition). Abingdon: Routledge.

Burman, E. (2008b) *Developments: Child, Image, Nation*. Abingdon: Routledge.

Burman, E. (2010) 'Explicating the tactics of banal exclusion: A British example', in I. Palmary, E. Burman, K. Chantler and P. Kiguwa (eds) *Gender and Migration: Feminist Interventions*. London: Zed Books.

Burman, E. and MacLure, M. (2005) 'Deconstruction as a method of research', in B. Somekh and C. Lewin (eds) *Research Methods in the Social Sciences*. London: Sage.

Burman, E. and Parker, I. (eds) (1993) *Discourse Analytic Research: Repertoires and Readings of Texts in Action*. London: Routledge.

Burman, E., Aitken, G., Alldred, P., Allwood, R., Billington, T., Goldberg, B., Gordo-López, Á.J., Heenan, C., Marks, D. and Warner, S. (1996) *Psychology Discourse Practice: From Regulation to Resistance*. London: Taylor and Francis.

Burr, V. (2003) *Social Constructionism* (second edition). London/New York: Routledge.

Buss, A.R. (1975) 'The emerging field of the sociology of psychological knowledge', *American Psychologist*, 30(10), 988–1002.

Butler, J. (1997) *Excitable Speech: A Politics of the Performative*. London: Routledge.

Butler, J., Laclau, E. and Žižek, S. (2000) *Contingency, Hegemony, Universality: Contemporary Dialogues on the Left*. London: Verso.

Callinicos, A. (1995) *Theories and Narratives: Reflections on the Philosophy of History*. Cambridge: Polity Press.

Cameron, D. (1995) *Verbal Hygiene*. London: Routledge.

Carpentier, N. and De Cleen, B. (2007) 'Bringing discourse theory into Media Studies: The applicability of Discourse Theoretical Analysis (DTA) for the study of media practices and discourses', *Journal of Language and Politics*, 6(2), 265–293.

Chandler, D. (2007) *Semiotics: The Basics* (second edition). Abingdon: Routledge.

Chomsky, N. (1959) 'Review of B.F. Skinner's *Verbal Behavior*', *Language*, 35(1), 26–58.

Chouliaraki, L. and Fairclough, N. (2000) *Discourse in Late Modernity*. Edinburgh: Edinburgh University Press.

Collier, A. (1994) *Critical Realism: An Introduction to Roy Bhaskar's Philosophy*. London: Verso.

Coward, R. and Ellis, J. (1977) *Language and Materialism: Developments in Semiology and the Theory of the Subject*. London: Routledge and Kegan Paul.

Creed, B. (1987) 'From here to modernity: Feminism and postmodernism', *Postmodernism Screen*, 28(2), 47–67.

Cresswell, M. and Spandler, H. (2009) 'Psychopolitics: Peter Sedgwick's legacy for the politics of mental health', *Social Theory and Health*, 7(2), 129–147.

Crossley, M. (2000) *Introducing Narrative Psychology: Self, Trauma and the Construction of Meaning*. Buckingham: Open University Press.

Čufer, E. and Irwin (1992) 'NSK state in time', in I. Arns (ed.) (2003) *IRWINRETROPRINCIP: 1983–2003*. Frankfurt: Revolver.

Curt, B. (1994) *Textuality and Tectonics: Troubling Social and Psychological Science*. Buckingham: Open University Press.

Cushman, P. (1991) 'Ideology obscured: Political uses of the self in Daniel Stern's infant', *American Psychologist*, 46(3), 206–219.

Danziger, K. (1985) 'The methodological imperative in psychology', *Philosophy of the Social Sciences*, 15, 1–13.

Dashtipour, P. (2012) *Social Identity in Question: Construction, Subjectivity and Critique*. Abingdon: Routledge.

Davies, B. and Harré, R. (1990) '"Positioning": The discursive production of selves', *Journal for the Theory of Social Behaviour*, 20(1), 43–63.

De Vos, J. (2012) *Psychologisation in Times of Globalisation*. Abingdon: Routledge.

Deleuze, G. and Guattari, F. (1977) *Anti-Oedipus: Capitalism and Schizophrenia*. New York: Viking.

Eagleton, T. (1985) 'Capitalism, modernism and postmodernism', *New Left Review*, 152, 60–73.

Eagleton, T. (1991) *Ideology: An Introduction*, London: Verso.

Easthope, A. (1990) '"I gotta use words when I talk to you": Deconstructing the theory of communication', in I. Parker and J. Shotter (eds) *Deconstructing Social Psychology*. London: Routledge.

Edwards, D. (1992) *Discourse and Cognition*. London: Sage.

Edwards, D. (1995) 'A commentary on discursive and critical psychology', *Culture & Psychology*, 1(1), 55–63.

Edwards, D. (1997) *Discourse and Cognition*. London: Sage.

Edwards, D. and Potter, J. (1992) *Discursive Psychology*. London: Sage.
Edwards, D., Ashmore, M. and Potter, J. (1995) 'Death and furniture: The rhetoric, politics and theology of bottom line arguments against relativism', *History of the Human Sciences*, 8(2), 25–49.
Elliott, A. (1992) *Social Theory and Psychoanalysis in Transition: Self and Society from Freud to Kristeva*. Cambridge: Polity Press.
Fairclough, N. (1989) *Language and Power*. London: Longman.
Farr, R.M. and Moscovici, S. (eds) (1984) *Social Representations*. Cambridge: Cambridge University Press.
Figueroa, H. and López, M. (1991) 'Commentary on discourse analysis', in E. Burman and I. Parker (eds) *Discourse Analytic Research: Repertoires and Readings of Texts in Action*. London: Routledge.
Filmer, P. (1972) 'On Harold Garfinkel's ethnomethodology', in P. Filmer, M. Phillipson, D. Silverman and D. Walsh (eds) *New Directions in Sociological Theory*. London: Collier/Macmillan.
Finlay, L. and Gough, B. (eds) (2003) *Reflexivity: A Practical Guide for Researchers in Health and Social Sciences*. Oxford: Blackwell.
Forrester, J. (1980) *Language and the Origins of Psychoanalysis*. London: Macmillan.
Foucault, M. (1966/1970) *The Order of Things*. London: Tavistock.
Foucault, M. (1969/1972) *The Archaeology of Knowledge*. London: Tavistock.
Foucault, M. (1975) *The Birth of the Clinic*. New York: Random House.
Foucault, M. (1975/1977) *Discipline and Punish*. London: Allen Lane.
Foucault, M. (1976/1981) *The History of Sexuality, Vol. I: An Introduction*. Harmondsworth: Pelican.
Foucault, M. (1977) *Language, Counter-Memory, Practice: Selected Essays and Interviews*. Oxford: Blackwell.
Foucault, M. (1980) *Power/Knowledge Selected Interviews and Other Writings 1972–1977*. Hassocks: Harvester Press.
Foulkes, S.H. (1964) *Therapeutic Group Analysis*. London: Allen and Unwin.
Freud, S. (1953–1974) *The Standard Edition of the Complete Psychological Works of Sigmund Freud* (24 vols) (translated by J. Strachey). London: Vintage, The Hogarth Press and the Institute of Psycho-Analysis.
Frosh, S. (1991) *Identity Crisis: Modernity, Psychoanalysis and the Self*. London: Macmillan.
Frosh, S. (2002) *After Words: The Personal in Gender, Culture and Psychotherapy*. Basingstoke/New York: Palgrave Macmillan.
Fruggeri, L. (1992) 'Therapeutic process as the social construction of change', in S. McNamee and K.J. Gergen (eds) *Therapy as Social Construction*. London: Sage.
Fussell, J. (2004) 'The Izbrisani (erased residents) issue in Slovenia', http://www.preventgenocide.org/europe/slovenia/ (accessed March 9, 2006).
Garfinkel, H. (1967) *Studies in Ethnomethodology*. New York: Prentice-Hall.
Gay, P. (1988) *Freud: A Life for Our Time*. New York: Norton.
Geras, N. (1987) 'Post-Marxism?', *New Left Review*, 163, 40–82.
Geras, N. (1995) 'Language, truth and justice', *New Left Review*, 209, 110–135.
Gergen, K.J. (1985) 'The social constructionist movement in modern psychology', *American Psychologist*, 40(3), 266–275.

Gergen, K.J. (1994) *Realities and Relationships*. Cambridge, MA: Harvard University Press.

Gergen, K.J. and Gergen, M.M. (1995) 'Relationalia: A hyperlogue'. Paper delivered at the Understanding the Social World, Huddersfield, UK, September.

Gill, R. (1995) 'Relativism, reflexivity and politics: Interrogating discourse analysis from a feminist perspective', in C. Kitzinger and S. Wilkinson (eds) *Discourse and Feminism*. London: Sage.

Glaser, B. and Strauss, A. (1967) *The Discovery of Grounded Theory: Strategies for Qualitative Research*. New York: Aldine.

Glynos, J. (2001) 'The grip of ideology: A Lacanian approach to the theory of ideology', *Journal of Political Ideologies*, 6(2), 191–214.

Glynos, J. and Howarth, D. (2007) *Logics of Critical Explanation in Social and Political Theory*. Abingdon: Routledge.

Goffman, E. (1979) *Gender Advertisements*. London: Macmillan.

Gordo, A. and De Vos, J. (eds) (2010) *Psychologisation Under Scrutiny (Special Issue)*. *Annual Review of Critical Psychology*, 8.

Gough, B. and McFadden, M. (2001) *Critical Social Psychology: An Introduction*. London: Palgrave.

Gramsci, A. (1971) *Selections from the Prison Notebooks*. London: Lawrence and Wishart.

Grünbaum, A. (1984) *The Foundations of Psychoanalysis: A Philosophical Investigation*. Berkeley, CA: University of California Press.

Gržnic, M. (2004) *Situated Contemporary Art Practices: Art, Theory and Activism from (the East of) Europe*. Ljubljana: Založba ZRC.

Habermas, J. (1972) *Knowledge and Human Interests*. London: Heinemann.

Hansen, A. (2005) 'A practical task: Ethnicity as a resource in social interaction', *Research on Language and Social Interaction*, 38(1), 63–104.

Hansen, S., McHoul, A. and Rapley, M. (2003) *Beyond Help: A Consumer's Guide to Psychology*. Ross-on-Wye: PCCS.

Harding, S. (ed.) (2003) *The Feminist Standpoint Theory Reader: Intellectual and Political Controversies*. London: Routledge.

Harré, R. (1979) *Social Being: A Theory for Social Psychology*. Oxford: Blackwell.

Harré, R. (1981) 'The positivist-empiricist approach and its alternative', in P. Reason and J. Rowan (eds) *Human Inquiry: A Sourcebook of New Paradigm Research*. Chichester: Wiley.

Harré, R. (1983) *Personal Being: A Theory for Individual Psychology*. Oxford: Blackwell.

Harré, R. (1986a) *Varieties of Realism: A Rationale for the Natural Sciences*. Oxford: Blackwell.

Harré, R. (ed.) (1986b) *The Social Construction of Emotions*. Oxford: Blackwell.

Harré, R. (1992) 'What is real in psychology: A plea for persons', *Theory and Psychology*, 2(2), 153–158.

Harré, R. (1995) 'Review of M. Douglas and D. Hull, *How Classification Works*', *Common Knowledge*, 4(3), 157–159.

Harré, R. (2004) 'Staking our claim for qualitative psychology as science', *Qualitative Research in Psychology*, 1(1), 3–14.

Harré, R. and Gillett, G. (1994) *The Discursive Mind*. London: Sage.
Harré, R. and Secord, P.F. (1972) *The Explanation of Social Behaviour*. Oxford: Blackwell.
Heelas, P. and Lock, A. (eds) (1981) *Indigenous Psychologies: The Anthropology of the Self*. London: Academic Press.
Henriques, J., Hollway, W., Urwin, C., Venn, C. and Walkerdine, V. (1998) *Changing the Subject: Psychology, Social Regulation and Subjectivity*. London: Routledge.
Henwood, K.L. and Pidgeon, N.F. (1992) 'Qualitative research and psychological theorizing', *British Journal of Psychology*, 83(1), 97–111.
Hepburn, A. (1999) 'Derrida and psychology: Deconstruction and its ab/uses in critical and discursive psychologies', *Theory & Psychology*, 9(5), 641–667.
Hepburn, A. (2004) 'Crying: Notes on description, transcription, and interaction', *Research on Language and Social Interaction*, 37(3), 251–290.
Hepburn, A. and Wiggins, S. (2007) *Discursive Research in Practice: New Approaches to Psychology and Interaction*. Cambridge: Cambridge University Press.
Heritage, J. (1984) *Garfinkel and Ethnomethodology*. Cambridge: Polity Press.
Hester, S. and Eglin, P. (eds) (1997) *Culture in Action: Studies in Membership Categorization Analysis*. Washington, DC: International Institute for Ethnomethodology and Conversation Analysis and University Press of America.
Hobson, R. (1985) *Forms of Feeling: The Heart of Psychotherapy*. London: Tavistock.
Hodge, R. and Kress, G. (1988) *Social Semiotics*. Cambridge: Polity Press.
Hollway, W. (1989) *Subjectivity and Method in Psychology: Gender, Meaning and Science*, London: Sage.
Hollway, W. and Jefferson, T. (2000) *Doing Qualitative Research Differently: Free Association, Narrative and the Interview Method*. London: Sage.
Hook, D. (2007) *Foucault, Psychology and the Analytics of Power*. London: Palgrave.
Hook, D. (2011) *A Critical Psychology of the Postcolonial: The Mind of Apartheid*. Abingdon: Routledge.
Hook, D. and Parker, I. (2002) 'Deconstruction, psychopathology and dialectics', *South African Journal of Psychology*, 32(2), 49–54.
Howarth, D., Norval, A. and Stavrakakis Y. (eds) (2000) *Discourse Theory and Political Analysis: Identities, Hegemonies and Social Change*. Manchester: Manchester University Press.
Hudson, B. (1984) 'Femininity and adolescence', in A. McRobbie and M. Nava (eds) *Gender and Generation*. Basingstoke: Macmillan.
Hunt, J. (1989) *Psychoanalytic Aspects of Fieldwork*. London: Sage.
Jacoby, R. (1983) *The Repression of Psychoanalysis*. New York: Basic Books.
Jeffs, N. (1995) 'Transnational dialogue in times of war: The peace movement in ex-Yugoslavia', *Radical Philosophy*, 73, 2–4.
Jung, C.G. (1983) *Jung: Selected Writings*. London: Fontana Press.
Kagan, C. and Burton, M. (2000) 'Prefigurative action research: An alternative basis for critical psychology?', *Annual Review of Critical Psychology*, 2, 73–87.

Kendall, G. and Michael, M. (1997) 'Politicizing the politics of postmodern social psychology', *Theory & Psychology*, 7(1), 7–29.
Kitzinger, C. (2000) 'Doing feminist conversation analysis', *Feminism & Psychology*, 10(2), 163–193.
Kvale, S. (ed.) (1992) *Psychology and Postmodernism*. London: Sage.
Lacan, J. (2006) *Écrits: The First Complete Edition in English* (translated with notes by B. Fink in collaboration with H. Fink and R. Grigg). New York: Norton.
Laclau, E. and Mouffe, C. (1985) *Hegemony and Socialist Strategy: Towards a Radical Democratic Politics*. London: Verso.
LAMHA (London Alliance for Mental Health Action) (1988) 'Community Treatment Orders 3: Statement', *Asylum: A Magazine for Democratic Psychiatry*, 12(3), 5–7.
Langer, M. (1989) *From Vienna to Managua*. London: Free Association Books.
Laplanche, J. (1989) *New Foundations for Psychoanalysis*. Oxford: Blackwell.
Latour, B. (2012) *On the Modern Cult of the Factish Gods*. Durham, NC: Duke University Press.
Lawson, D. (1988) 'Community Treatment Orders 1: The problem', *Asylum: A Magazine for Democratic Psychiatry*, 12(3), 3–4.
Levett, A. (1994) 'Problems of cultural imperialism in the study of child sexual abuse' in I. Parker (ed.) (2011) *Critical Psychology: Critical Concepts in Psychology, Volume 3, Dominant Models of Psychology and Their Limits*. Abingdon/New York: Routledge, pp. 279–307.
Lomas, P. (1977) *Against Interpretation: What's Wrong with Psychoanalysis?* Harmondsworth: Pelican.
London Psychogeographical Association (1997) 'Luther Blissett Three-sided Football League', in S. Home (ed.) *Mind Invaders: A Reader in Psychic Warfare, Cultural Sabotage and Semiotic Terrorism*. London: Serpent's Tail.
Lovibond, S. (1989) 'Feminism and postmodernism', *New Left Review*, 178, 5–28.
Lowe, R. (1999) 'Between the "no longer" and the "not yet": Postmodernism as a context for critical therapeutic work', in I. Parker (ed.) *Deconstructing Psychotherapy*. London: Sage.
Lyotard, J.-F. (1979/1984) *The Postmodern Condition: A Report on Knowledge*. Manchester: Manchester University Press.
Magaš, B. (1993) *The Destruction of Yugoslavia: Tracking the Break-up 1980–92*. London: Verso.
Marsh, P., Rosser, E. and Harré, R. (1974) *The Rules of Disorder*. London: Routledge and Kegan Paul.
Masson, J.M. (1992) *Final Analysis: The Making and Unmaking of a Psychoanalyst*. London: HarperCollins.
McHoul, A. and Rapley, M. (2005) 'A case of attention-deficit/hyperactivity disorder diagnosis: Sir Karl and Francis B. slug it out on the consulting room floor', *Discourse and Society*, 16(3), 419–449.
McKenzie, W. and Monk, G. (1997) 'Learning and teaching narrative ideas', in G. Monk, J. Winslade, K. Crocket and D. Epston (eds) *Narrative Therapy in Practice: The Archaeology of Hope*. San Francisco, CA: Jossey-Bass.
McNamee, S. and Gergen, K.J. (eds) (1992) *Therapy as Social Construction*. London: Sage.

Middleton, D. and Edwards, D. (eds) (1990) *Collective Remembering*. London: Sage.
Monk, G., Winslade, J., Crocket, K. and Epston, D. (eds) (1997) *Narrative Therapy in Practice: The Archaeology of Hope*. San Francisco, CA: Jossey-Bass.
Monroe, A. (2005) *Interrogation Machine: Laibach and the NSK State*. Cambridge, MA: MIT Press.
Moore, S. (1988) 'Getting a bit of the other: The pimps of postmodernism', in R. Chapman and J. Rutherford (eds) *Male Order: Unwrapping Masculinity*. London: Lawrence and Wishart.
Moscovici, S. (1976/2008) *Psychoanalysis: Its Image and Its Public*. Cambridge: Polity Press.
Mudrak, M. (2001) 'Neue Slowenische Kunst and the Semiotics of Suprematism', in I. Arns (ed.) (2003) *IRWINRETROPRINCIP: 1983–2003*. Frankfurt: Revolver.
Neill, C. (2015) *Ethics and Psychology: Beyond Codes of Practice*. Abingdon: Routledge.
Newman, F. and Holzman, L. (1996) *Unscientific Psychology: A Cultural-Performatory Approach to Understanding Human Life*. Westport, CT: Praeger.
Newman, F. and Holzman, L. (1997) *The End of Knowing (And a New Developmental Way of Learning)*. London: Routledge.
Norris, C. (1996) *Reclaiming Truth: Contribution to a Critique of Cultural Relativism*. London: Lawrence and Wishart.
Parker, I. (1988) 'Deconstructing accounts', in I. Parker (2014) *Psychology After Deconstruction: Erasure and Social Reconstruction*. Abingdon: Routledge.
Parker, I. (1989) *The Crisis in Modern Social Psychology, and How to End it*. London: Routledge.
Parker, I. (1992a) *Discourse Dynamics: Critical Analysis for Social and Individual Psychology*, London: Routledge.
Parker, I. (1992b) 'Discourse discourse: Social psychology and postmodernity', in J. Doherty, E. Graham and M. Malek (eds) *Postmodernism and the Social Sciences*. London: Macmillan.
Parker, I. (1993) 'Social constructionist psychoanalysis and the real', in B. Kaplan, L. Mos, H. Stam and W. Thorngate (eds) *Recent Trends in Theoretical Psychology (Vol. III)*. New York: Springer.
Parker, I. (1994) 'Reflexive research and the grounding of analysis: Social psychology and the psy-complex', *Journal of Community and Applied Social Psychology*, 4(4), 239–252.
Parker, I. (1995) 'Masculinity and cultural change: Wild men', *Culture & Psychology*, 1(4), 455–475.
Parker, I. (1996) 'Discursive psychology', in D. Fox and I. Prilleltensky (eds) *Critical Psychology: An Introductory Handbook*. London: Sage.
Parker, I. (1997) *Psychoanalytic Culture: Psychoanalytic Discourse in Western Society*. London: Sage.
Parker, I. (1998a) 'Against postmodernism: Psychology in cultural context', *Theory & Psychology*, 8(5), 621–647.
Parker, I. (ed.) (1998b) *Social Constructionism, Discourse and Realism*. London: Sage.

Parker, I. (1999a) 'Against relativism in psychology, on balance', *History of the Human Sciences*, 12(4), 61–78.
Parker, I. (1999b) 'Critical reflexive humanism and critical constructionist psychology', in D.J. Nightingale and J. Cromby (eds) *Social Constructionist Psychology: A Critical Analysis*. Buckingham: Open University Press.
Parker, I. (ed.) (1999c) *Deconstructing Psychotherapy*. London: Sage.
Parker, I. (2002) *Critical Discursive Psychology*. London: Palgrave Macmillan.
Parker, I. (2004) 'Discursive practice: Analysis, context and action in critical research', *International Journal of Critical Psychology*, 10, 150–173.
Parker, I. (2005a) *Qualitative Psychology: Introducing Radical Research*. Buckingham: Open University Press.
Parker, I. (2005b) 'Laibach and enjoy: Slovenian theory and practice', *Psychoanalysis, Culture & Society*, 10, 105–112.
Parker, I. (2007a) *Revolution in Psychology: Alienation to Emancipation*. London: Pluto Press.
Parker, I. (2007b) 'The truth about overidentification', in P. Bowman and R. Stamp (eds) *The Truth of Žižek*. New York: Continuum.
Parker, I. (2008) 'Emotional illiteracy: Margins of resistance', *Qualitative Research in Psychology*, 5(1), 19–32.
Parker, I. (ed.) (2011a) *Critical Psychology: Critical Concepts in Psychology* (4 vols). Abingdon/New York: Routledge.
Parker, I. (2011b) *Lacanian Psychoanalysis: Revolutions in Subjectivity*. Abingdon: Routledge.
Parker, I. (2012) 'Discursive social psychology now', *British Journal of Social Psychology*, 51(3), 471–477
Parker, I. and Pavón Cuéllar, D. (eds) (2013) *Lacan, Discourse, Event: New Psychoanalytic Approaches to Textual Indeterminacy*. Abingdon: Routledge.
Parker, I. and Shotter, J. (eds) (1990) *Deconstructing Social Psychology*. London: Routledge.
Parker, I. and Spears, R. (eds) (1996) *Psychology and Society: Radical Theory and Practice*. London: Pluto Press.
Parker, I., Georgaca, E., Harper, D., Stowell-Smith, M. and McLaughlin, T. (1995) *Deconstructing Psychopathology*. London: Sage.
Pavón Cuéllar, D. (2010) *From the Conscious Interior to an Exterior Unconscious: Lacan, Discourse Analysis and Social Psychology*. London: Karnac.
Penley, C. (1989) '"A certain refusal of difference": Feminism and film theory', in C. Penley, *The Future of an Illusion*. London: Routledge.
Peräkylä, A., Antaki, C., Vehviläinen, S. and Leudar, I. (eds) (2008) *Conversation Analysis of Psychotherapy*. Cambridge: Cambridge University Press.
Potter, J. (1998) 'Fragments in the realization of relativism', in I. Parker (ed.) *Social Constructionism, Discourse and Realism*. London: Sage.
Potter, J. and Wetherell, M. (1987) *Discourse and Social Psychology: Beyond Attitudes and Behaviour*. London: Sage.
Potter, J., Wetherell, M., Gill, R. and Edwards, D. (1990) 'Discourse-noun, verb or social practice', *Philosophical Psychology*, 3(2), 205–217.

Prilleltensky, I. (1994) *The Morals and Politics of Psychology: Psychological Discourse and the Status Quo.* New York: State University of New York Press.

Ranciere, J. (1974/2011) *Althusser's Lesson.* New York: Continuum.

Rapley, M. (2012) 'Ethnomethodology/conversation analysis', in D. Harper and A. Thompson (eds) *Qualitative Research Methods in Mental Health and Psychotherapy: A Guide for Students and Practitioners.* Chichester: Wiley-Blackwell.

Reason, P. and Rowan, J. (eds) (1981) *Human Inquiry: A Sourcebook of New Paradigm Research.* Chichester: Wiley.

Reavey, P. (ed.) (2011) *Visual Methods in Psychology: Using and Interpreting Images in Qualitative Research.* Abingdon: Routledge.

Reicher, S.D. (1996) 'Self-categorization and group identity in discourse', in T. Ibañez and L. Iñiquez (eds) *Critical Social Psychology.* London: Sage.

Riegel, K.F. (1976) 'The dialectics of human development', *American Psychologist*, 31(10), 689–700.

Riley, D. (1983) *War in the Nursery: Theories of the Child and the Mother.* London: Virago.

Robbins, B. (1991) 'Tenured radicals, the new McCarthyism and "PC"', *New Left Review*, 188, 151–157.

Rorty, R. (1980) *Philosophy and the Mirror of Nature.* Oxford: Blackwell.

Rorty, R. (1989) *Contingency, Irony and Solidarity.* Cambridge: Cambridge University Press.

Rorty, R. (1992) 'We anti-representationalists', *Radical Philosophy*, 60, 40–42.

Rose, D., Efraim, D., Gervais, M., Joffe, H., Jovchelovitch, S. and Morant, N. (1995) 'Questioning consensus in social representations theory', *Papers on Social Representations*, 4(2), 150–176.

Rose, N. (1985) *The Psychological Complex: Psychology, Politics and Society in England 1869–1939.* London: Routledge and Kegan Paul.

Roiser, M. (1977) 'Postmodernism, postmodernity and social psychology', in T. Ibáñez and L. Iñiguez (eds) *Critical Social Psychology.* London: Sage.

Roudinesco, E. (1990) *Jacques Lacan and Co.: A History of Psycho-Analysis in France 1925–1985.* London: Free Association Books.

Sacks, H. (1972) 'On the analyzability of stories by children', in J. Gumperz and D. Hymes (eds) *Directions in Sociolinguistics: The Ethnography of Communication.* New York: Holt, Rinehart and Winston.

Sacks, H. (1992) *Lectures on Conversation.* Oxford: Blackwell.

Sacks, H., Schegloff, E.A. and Jefferson, G.A. (1974) 'A simplest systematics for the organization of turn-taking in conversation', *Language*, 50(4), 697–735.

Sarup, M. (1988) *An Introductory Guide to Post-structuralism and Postmodernism.* Hassocks: Harvester Wheatsheaf.

Saussure, F. de (1974) *Course in General Linguistics*, London: Fontana.

Sawyer, R. (2002) 'A discourse on discourse: An archeological history of an intellectual concept', *Cultural Studies*, 16(3), 433–456.

Seeman, M. (1971) 'The urban alienations: Some dubious themes from Marx to Marcuse', *Journal of Personality and Social Psychology*, 19(2), 63–84.

Shotter, J. (1984) *Social Accountability and Selfhood.* Oxford: Blackwell.

Shotter, J. (1993) *Conversational Realities: Studies in Social Constructionism*. London: Sage.
Skinner, B.F. (1957) *Verbal Behavior*. New York: Appleton-Century-Crofts.
Smith, D. (1978) 'K is mentally ill: The anatomy of a factual account', *Sociology*, 12(1), 23–53.
Smith, J., Flowers, P. and Larkin, M. (2009) *Interpretative Phenomenological Analysis: Theory, Method and Research*. London: Sage.
Spanke, D. (2003) 'Irwin doesn't believe in deer: Irwin's icons, kitsch, propaganda, and art', in I. Arns (ed.) *IRWINRETROPRINCIP: 1983–2003*. Frankfurt: Revolver.
Squire, C. (1990) 'Crisis, what crisis? Discourses and narratives of the "social" in social psychology', in I. Parker and J. Shotter (eds) *Deconstructing Social Psychology*. London: Routledge.
Squire, C. (ed.) (2000) *Culture in Psychology*. London: Routledge.
Stainton Rogers, R., Stenner, P., Gleeson, K. and Stainton Rogers, W. (1995) *Social Psychology: A Critical Agenda*. Cambridge: Polity Press.
Stavrakakis, Y. (2007) *The Lacanian Left: Psychoanalysis, Theory, Politics*. Edinburgh: Edinburgh University Press.
Stenner, P. (1993) 'Discoursing jealousy', in E. Burman and I. Parker (eds) *Discourse Analytic Research: Repertoires and Readings of Texts in Action*. London: Routledge.
Stenner, P. and Eccleston, C. (1994) 'On the textuality of being: Towards an invigorated social constructionism', *Theory & Psychology*, 4(1), 83–103.
Stepančič, L. (1994) 'The poster scandal: New Collectivism and the 1987 Youth Day', in I. Arns (ed.) (2003) *IRWINRETROPRINCIP: 1983–2003*. Frankfurt: Revolver.
Stern, D. (1985) *The Interpersonal World of the Infant*. New York: Basic Books.
Tiffany, D. (1990) 'Phantom transmissions: The radio broadcasts of Ezra Pound', *SubStance*, 19(1), 53–74
Timms, E. and Segal, N. (eds) (1988) *Freud in Exile: Psychoanalysis and its Vicissitudes*. New Haven, CT/London: Yale University Press.
Van Dijk, T. (2003) 'Critical discourse analysis', in D. Schiffrin, D. Tannen and H.E. Hamilton (eds) *Handbook of Discourse Analysis*. Oxford: Blackwell.
Van Leeuwen, T. and Wodak, R. (1999) 'Legitimizing immigration control: A discourse-historical analysis', *Discourse Studies*, 1(1), 83–118.
Voelklein, C. and Howarth, C. (2005) 'A review of controversies about social representations theory: A British debate', *Culture & Psychology*, 11(4), 431–454.
Vološinov, V. (1973) *Freudianism: A Philosophical Critique*. Boston, MA: MIT Press.
Walkerdine, V. (1981) 'Sex, power and pedagogy', *Screen Education*, 38, 14–21.
Walkerdine, V. (1988) *The Mastery of Reason: Cognitive Development and the Production of Rationality*. London: Routledge.
Weedon, C. (1987) *Feminist Practice and Poststructuralist Theory*. Oxford: Blackwell.
Wetherell, M. and Potter, J. (1992) *Mapping the Language of Racism: Discourse and the Legitimation of Exploitation*. Hemel Hempstead: Harvester Wheatsheaf.

Whelan, P. (2012) 'Oxymoronic and sociologically monstrous? Feminist conversation analysis', *Qualitative Research in Psychology*, 9(4), 279–291.
Williamson, J. (1978) *Decoding Advertisements: Ideology and Meaning in Advertising*. London: Marion Boyars.
Willig, C. (2001) *Introducing Qualitative Research in Psychology: Adventures in Theory and Method*. Buckingham: Open University Press.
Wittgenstein, L. (1958) *Philosophical Investigations*. Oxford: Basil Blackwell.
Wodak, R. and Chilton, P. (eds) (2005) *A New Agenda in (Critical) Discourse Analysis*. Amsterdam: Benjamins.
Wodak, R. and Matouschek, B. (1993) '"We are dealing with people whose origins one can clearly tell just by looking": Critical discourse analysis and the study of neo-racism in contemporary Austria', *Discourse and Society*, 4(2), 225–248.
Wolfenstein, E.V. (1991) 'On the uses and abuses of psychoanalysis in cultural research', *Free Associations*, 2(4), 515–547.
Woolgar, S. (ed.) (1988) *Knowledge and Reflexivity: New Frontiers in the Sociology of Knowledge*. London: Sage.
Wowk, M. (2007) 'Kitzinger's feminist conversation analysis: Critical observations', *Human Studies*, 30(2), 131–155.
Žižek, S. (1989) *The Sublime Object of Ideology*. London: Verso.
Žižek, S. (1990) 'Beyond discourse-analysis', in E. Laclau (ed.) *New Reflections on The Revolution of Our Time*. London: Verso.
Žižek, S. (1991) *For They Know Not What They Do: Enjoyment as a Political Factor*. London: Verso.
Žižek, S. (1993a) 'Why are Laibach and NSK not Fascists?' in I. Arns (ed.) (2003) *IRWINRETROPRINCIP: 1983–2003*. Frankfurt: Revolver.
Žižek, S. (1993b) 'Es gibt keinen Staat in Europa', in I. Arns (ed.) (2003) *IRWIN-RETROPRINCIP: 1983–2003*. Frankfurt: Revolver. Also available at http://www.medialounge.net/lounge/workspace/nettime/DOCS/1/staat.html (accessed 28 February 2014).
Žižek, S. (1994) 'The enlightenment in Laibach', in I. Arns (ed.) (2003) *IRWINRETROPRINCIP: 1983–2003*. Frankfurt: Revolver.

Index

abstraction 83, 84, 91, 93
academic imperialism 85–86
action research 16
Actor Network Theory 13
ADHD *see* attention-deficit/hyperactivity disorder
advertising 23
affect 26, 69
agency 1, 18, 21, 34, 47, 59
alienation 32
Althusser, Louis 23–24, 65, 71, 74
American Psychological Association (APA) 93
Anderson, H. 40
anti-humanism 21, 84
anti-realism 36, 37
anti-representationalists 37
APA *see* American Psychological Association
attention-deficit/hyperactivity disorder (ADHD) 20
Austin, J.L. 46
authorial responsibility 44, 54
'auto-discourse-analytic' research 104

Badiou, Alain 24
Barthes, Roland 54, 56
Baudrillard, Jean 35
behaviourism 3, 16, 44, 48
Benjamin, Walter 35
Bettelheim, B. 52–53, 57
Birth of the Nation 100
Blackburn, S. 92
'blank subjectivity' 44, 45, 46, 47–48
Blissett, L. 7

body 71, 72
Boring, E.G. 49
boundaries 5–6, 83
Burman, Erica 76
Butler, Judith 25

CA *see* Conversation Analysis
capitalism 5, 41–42, 92, 101, 102
CDA *see* Critical Discourse Analysis
children 68, 69, 70–72, 73, 75
choice 85–86
Chomsky, Noam 38
Churchill, Winston 103
cognitive psychology 3, 26, 30, 47
cognitive theory 19
cognitivism 84
coherence 20, 65
collective action 87–88
collective phenomena 44, 53–54
'collective unconscious' 53
Collier, A. 38
'common sense' 64, 66, 71, 84
communication 16
'complex subjectivity' 44, 59–60, 61
'conditions of possibility' 21, 24, 69
conflict 22
consensus 17
conspiracies 92, 95, 96, 103
construction 64, 66, 69
constructionism 1, 4, 51, 81–82; 'complex subjectivity' 59–60; critical relativism 33; discursive work 46; Political Discourse Theory 25; postmodernism 30, 85; power 31; psychoanalysis 62; 'turn to discourse' 28

Index

context: cultural 90; historical 58, 104; institutional and intellectual 42; social 8, 78
contradiction 17, 22, 55, 65
Conversation Analysis (CA) 10–12, 14, 20, 46, 47, 94–95; compared with ethnomethodology 12–13; correct explication 101; Critical Discourse Analysis linked to 19
correct explication 101–102
counter-discourse 21
counter-transference 56, 66, 67, 74
Critical Discourse Analysis (CDA) 18–20, 22, 24, 26
critical discursive practice 6
critical discursive psychology 3–4, 25
'critical distance' 69
critical psychology 6, 7, 10, 20, 27, 35, 93–94; 'blank subjectivity' 47; Conversation Analysis 11; discourse analysis linked with 9; Foucauldian Discourse Analysis 22; Lacanian Discourse Analysis 24; narrative 15; postmodernism 28, 29, 30, 38, 43; realism 38; Thematic Analysis 18
critical realism 38
critical reflection 39, 40
critical relativism 33
cultural practices 6, 7, 69
cultural studies 22, 51
culture 5, 64, 66, 90; 'complex subjectivity' 59–60; critical relativism 33; cultural specificity of analytic vocabularies 45, 58–59; discursive complexes 60, 61–62; postmodernism 38, 39, 85; psychoanalysis 51, 52, 62, 67, 73–74; social constructionism 81–82; Western 26, 45, 50, 51–52, 58, 59–60, 61, 66, 67
cyberspace 26

DARG *see* Discourse and Rhetoric Group
Dark Side of the Moon (Pink Floyd) 35
Davies, B. 74
'death of the author' 16, 54, 56
deconstruction 6, 64, 69; postmodernism 31, 32, 40; problems with discourse analysis 82

defences 57, 67, 74
Deleuze, Gilles 59, 63, 73, 74
Derrida, Jacques 32
development 33
developmental psychology 32, 50
DHA *see* Discourse Historical Analysis
diagnosis 20
'dialectical reversals' 41
dialectics 32
difference 55, 87–88
disciplinary segregation 102–104
discourse 1, 18, 46, 79; assumptions 6; 'complex subjectivity' 59; culture 67; Foucauldian Discourse Analysis 21; Political Discourse Theory 24; politics 86–88; reductionism 84; reification of 83; 'turn to' 1, 2–3, 28, 93, 94; *see also* repertoires
discourse analysis 3, 4–7, 8–10; collective phenomena 53; correct explication 101–102; 'critical distance' 69; disciplinary segregation 102–104; eight approaches to 9–27; everyday conversation 96–97; formal sequences 99–101; interpersonal interaction 97–99; postmodern psychology 28, 31–32; problems with 76–90, 91, 93–94, 96–105; psychoanalysis 44–46, 51–52, 56, 60, 62, 63; reflexivity 39; role of 93; subjectivity 47
Discourse and Rhetoric Group (DARG) 4
Discourse Historical Analysis (DHA) 19
Discourse Theoretical Analysis (DTA) 19
Discourse Unit 1, 8
discursive complexes 60–62, 63–75
'discursive culture' 5
discursive position 21, 88
discursive practice 6, 7, 91–92, 97, 99, 104–105
discursive psychology 46, 47, 94; critical 3–4, 25; psychoanalysis and 49–50, 51–52, 54
'dissidence' 97, 101
dreams 38–39, 56

DTA *see* Discourse Theoretical Analysis

Eagleton, Terry 33, 37
Eccleston, C. 33
ego-psychology 58
EM *see* ethnomethodology
emotion 11, 26, 30, 33
empiricism 48, 49, 90;
  Conversation Analysis 11, 20;
  ethnomethodological 47; problems
  with discourse analysis 81–86;
  Thematic Analysis 17
England 103–104
'enigmatic signifiers' 72
Enlightenment 1, 41
essentialism 49
ethics 26, 78
ethnomethodology (EM) 12–14, 46, 47, 101
'ethogenic' social psychology 31
Europe 32, 104, 105
everyday conversation 96–97
experience 50, 61
exploitation 7

'facts' 8–9, 58
family therapy 40
FANI *see* Free Associative Narrative Inquiry
fascism 20, 96, 98, 100, 101, 103
FCA *see* Feminist Conversation Analysis
FDA *see* Foucauldian Discourse Analysis
feminism: difference 87; discourse analysis 89; ethnomethodology 13; 'interpretive vigilance' 80; Political Discourse Theory 25; politics of deconstruction 31; postmodernism 42
Feminist Conversation Analysis (FCA) 11, 20
Fenichel, Otto 50
FIAT 96, 100
Figueroa Sarriera, Heidi 76, 78–79, 80, 90
'floating signifiers' 24–25
formal sequences 99–101
Foucauldian Discourse Analysis (FDA) 20–22, 94

Foucault, Michel 20–21, 22, 26, 40, 64, 88
Foulkes, S.H. 53
France 58, 60
Frankfurt school 50
Free Associative Narrative Inquiry (FANI) 15, 23
Freud, Sigmund 24, 44, 51, 52, 53, 57–58, 70
Fruggeri, L. 40
function 64, 65, 69
fundamentalism 41

Gallagher, Liam 29, 42
Garfinkel, Harold 12, 13
gaze 75, 91, 93, 97
gender 11, 25, 70, 80
generalization 77
Geras, N. 36
Gergen, Ken 31, 41
Gergen, Mary 42
Germany 58
Gill, Ros 76
'Glop Art' 7
Goolishian, H. 40
Grounded Theory 17, 48
grounding devices 36–37
Grünbaum, A. 52
The Guardian 29, 42
Guattari, Félix 59, 63, 73, 74

Habermas, J. 52–53, 57, 58
Harré, Rom 30, 31, 37, 59–60, 74, 81
hegemony 25
hermeneutics 57
historicism 84
history 3, 4, 18, 21, 99;
  postmodernism 33, 34, 35;
  textuality 55
human science 44, 52–53
humanism 16, 21, 30, 48, 54;
  experience 50; 'uncomplicated subjectivity' 44, 46, 48

idealism 79
identity 25, 38, 39, 47, 102, 105;
  see also self
ideology: Althusser 71, 74; critical psychology 38; discursive complexes 74; dominant 91;

ideology (*cont.*):
  Foucauldian Discourse Analysis 21;
  North American 50; NSK 97,
  98–99, 101, 105; Political Discourse
  Theory 24; popular culture 64;
  postmodernism 33–34; problems
  with discourse analysis 82–83;
  Rorty 36, 37; Semiotic Analysis 23
images 22, 23
imperialism 85–86
institutions: ego-psychology 58;
  hermeneutics 57; institutional
  context 42; power 27, 88; rules
  of 85
intellectual context 42
International Psychoanalytical
  Association (IPA) 49, 50, 56
interpellation 23, 65
interpersonal interaction 97–99
interpretation 15, 16, 88, 89, 92, 102
Interpretative Phenomenological
  Analysis 17
'interpretative repertoires' 14, 48, 60
'interpretive vigilance' 80
IPA *see* International Psychoanalytical
  Association
Italy 100

Jung, C.G. 53

Kendall, G. 41
Kensit, Patsy 29, 42
Klein, Melanie 15
knowledge: 'crisis of' 90; discursive
  complexes 72, 74; dominant
  forms of 96; empiricism 81;
  ethnomethodology 12; Foucauldian
  Discourse Analysis 21; institutional
  context 42; psychoanalysis 45,
  60; psychology as shared system
  of 37; readers 80; sociology of
  scientific 4, 14

laboratory experiments 2, 30
Lacan, Jacques 22, 23, 24, 44, 51, 53, 58
Lacanian Discourse Analysis
  (LDA) 23, 24
Laclau, Ernesto 24
Laibach 96–105
Langer, Marie 50

language 5, 6, 9, 27, 46, 47, 93;
  'common sense' 64; discursive
  complexes 61, 63, 71, 74;
  inconsistency 54; Lacanian
  Discourse Analysis 24; oppression
  maintained in 80; Political Discourse
  Theory 25; psychoanalysis 45,
  51, 57–58; Semiotic Analysis 23;
  signification 88; social relations 79;
  'turn to' 1, 28, 30, 90; as verbal
  behaviour 2–3, 16; *see also*
  discourse
Laplanche, J. 72, 74
Latour, Bruno 13
Law 70–71, 74
LDA *see* Lacanian Discourse Analysis
liberal democracy 37
liberal pluralism 32, 87
linguistics 18, 19
literary theory 16, 32, 54
London Psychogeographical
  Association 7
López, María Milagros 76, 78–79, 80, 90
Lowe, R. 41
Luria, A.R. 49
Lyotard, J.-F. 33, 34

Macnaghten, Phil 76
Malevich, Kazimir 100
Marks, Deborah 76
Marshall, Harriet 76
Marx, Karl 24
Marxism 18, 30, 32, 37
material culture 73
MCA *see* Membership Categorization
  Analysis
McKenzie, W. 40
meaning 18, 49, 54; construction
  of 66; discursive complexes 67;
  Interpretative Phenomenological
  Analysis 17; postmodernism 38, 39;
  problems with discourse analysis 84;
  relativism 87; variation 65
Membership Categorization Analysis
  (MCA) 10, 12
memory 47, 55
mental health 13, 86
method 2, 4, 10, 20, 90; problems
  of 77–81; psychoanalytic 66–67;
  Thematic Analysis 16

Michael, M. 41
'micronations' 91, 105
micro-sociology 10, 12, 13
'modern singularity' 41–42
modernism 33
modernity 34, 85
Monk, G. 40
Moscovici, S. 60
motivation 47
Mouffe, Chantal 24

NA *see* Narrative Analysis
narrative 14, 15, 33, 41, 79
Narrative Analysis (NA) 14–16
narrative therapy 15, 41
neoliberalism 5, 27, 92
Neue Slowenische Kunst (NSK) 97–105
neuropsychology 47
'new paradigm' 1, 30, 31, 32
New Slovenian Art (NSK) 97–105
normality 63, 86
NSK *see Neue Slowenische Kunst*

Oasis 29
object relations theory 50
objectivity 32, 56, 94
Oedipal triangle 70–71
opportunity 33, 34
oppression 13, 32, 35; feminism 80, 89; psychology 52–53; Rorty on 37
Opus Dei (Laibach) 96–97, 98, 100, 103
other/Other 45, 53, 56–57

'paradigm shifts' 28
Parker, Ian 41, 68, 93
pathology 15, 20, 21, 63
PDT *see* Political Discourse Theory
performativity 79
phenomenology 12, 17
Piaget, Jean 49
Pink Floyd 35
Political Discourse Theory (PDT) 22, 24–25
politics 31, 34; avoidance of 91, 102–103; NSK 101–102, 103–104, 105; political struggle 92, 104; problems with discourse analysis 82–83, 86–88, 89; *see also* the state

popular culture 64
positivism 2, 19, 50, 55
postmodernism 1, 4, 28–43; capitalist culture 41–42; contemporary culture 85; 'extremely unlikely story theory' 35–36; ideology 33–34; 'naked commercialism story' 32–33; power 31–32; psychology and 34–35, 37–38, 43; and the real world 36–37, 38; reflexivity 39–40; therapy 40, 41
post-structuralism 1, 46, 64, 79, 86; literary theory 16; psychoanalysis 51; Semiotic Analysis 22; 'turn to language' 90; 'uncomplicated subjectivity' 49
Pound, Ezra 100, 101–102, 103
power 18, 73, 86, 88; academic institutions 27; 'common sense' 64; Conversation Analysis 11; Critical Discourse Analysis 19, 20; critical psychology 38; critical reflection 40; cultural practices 69; deconstructive therapy 40; discursive complexes 74; feminist 'standpoint' perspective 13; Foucauldian Discourse Analysis 21, 22; interpersonal interaction 98; materiality of 79–80; NSK 105; postmodernism 31–32; psychoanalysis 51; reductionism 84; researchers 78, 80, 102–103; sites for the relay of 91–92, 99; texts 54, 55, 57, 58
pragmatism 36, 40
progress 33, 34, 35
psychoanalysis 1–2, 44–62; collective phenomena 53–54; 'complex subjectivity' 61; 'conditions of possibility' 69; cultural specificity 58–59; discursive approaches 51–52; discursive complexes 60–62, 63, 67, 70–75; as form of reading 54; Foucault 64; human science 52–53; Lacanian 24, 44, 50, 55, 56, 58–59, 74; as language 57–58; memory and history as textuality 54–55; method 66–67; Narrative Analysis 15; problems with discourse

psychoanalysis (*cont.*):
  analysis 80–81; regulation
  of children 75; researcher
  subjectivity 55–56; selfhood 66;
  Semiotic Analysis 22, 23; the
  subject 26; subject positions 65;
  text as 'other' 56–57
'psychological culture' 5, 7
psychologization 5, 6, 18, 26–27, 103
psychotherapy *see* therapy
'psy-complex' 5, 32, 34, 75

qualitative research 3, 77; Grounded
  Theory 17; reflexivity 26;
  subjectivity 56; 'uncomplicated
  subjectivity' 48–49
quantitative research 2
Queen of England 92
queer theory 25

Raabe, Bianca 76
race 25
racism 19
rationality 93
realism 4, 9, 31, 33, 35, 36–37, 38, 43
reality principle 71
reductionism 54, 56, 78, 84, 91, 93
reflection 33, 34, 42, 59
reflexivity 4, 26, 37; Critical Discourse
  Analysis 19; postmodernism 39–40;
  problem of 88; psychoanalysis 53;
  relativism 83
Reich, Wilhelm 50
reification of discourse 83
relativism 4, 25, 79; critical
  psychology 38; discursive 55;
  'new paradigm' 30, 31; politics 87;
  postmodernism 28, 31, 33, 35–36;
  problems with discourse analysis 83
repertoires 61, 90, 101;
  interpretative 14, 48, 60; problems
  with discourse analysis 77, 78, 79;
  see also discourse
representation 17, 65, 88, 91–92, 99,
  101
reproduction 9, 10
researchers: position of 19, 26, 63,
  75, 89; power 78, 80, 102–103;
  reflexivity 88; sensitivity 66;
  subjectivity 45, 49, 55–56, 64

resistance 7, 34, 59; critical
  reflection 40; discursive
  complexes 73, 74; Foucauldian
  Discourse Analysis 21; intellectual
  context 42; problem of 88
respecification 11, 12
Rorty, Richard 36–37
Russia 100

SA *see* Semiotic Analysis
Sacks, Harvey 10, 11, 14
Saussure, Ferdinand de 55
'schizoanalysis' 59
'schizophrenia' 73, 74
science 28, 30; critical relativism 33;
  human science 44, 52–53; as social
  construction 4; war over scientific
  paradigms 93
scientific psychology 99
Secord, P.F. 30, 37
self 30, 41, 42, 46, 65; 'blank
  subjectivity' 47; discursive
  complexes 60, 61; nation and 92;
  North American ideology 50;
  psychoanalysis 45, 53, 58–59;
  'uncomplicated subjectivity' 48;
  Western culture 59; *see also*
  identity; subjectivity
self-reference 45, 50, 88
Semiotic Analysis (SA) 22–24
sexuality 11, 72
Shotter, J. 59–60
signifiers 7, 24–25, 72
signs 22, 66
singularity 41–42
Slovenia 58, 96–97, 98–99, 100, 102,
  104
social constructionism 1, 4, 51, 81–82;
  'complex subjectivity' 59–60;
  critical relativism 33; discursive
  work 46; Political Discourse
  Theory 25; postmodernism 30, 85;
  power 31; psychoanalysis 62; 'turn
  to discourse' 28
social context 8, 78
social psychology 14, 18, 30, 32, 64;
  'ethogenic' 31; psychoanalysis 51;
  reductionism 78; the subject 50;
  'uncomplicated subjectivity' 49
social relations 30, 79

Index

'social representations' 17, 18, 47, 60, 62
social structures 37, 59
social worlds 1, 12
sociology 12, 17, 48
sociology of scientific knowledge 4, 13
speech 26–27, 48
Spielrein, Sabina 49
'standpoint' perspective 13
the state 28, 92, 102, 105
Stenner, Paul 33, 76
Stern, Daniel 50
stories 1, 15, 41, 79
'story metaphor' 40
'story-theories' 28–29
structuralism 1, 16, 22, 46, 47
structure 9, 29, 42, 57
'subject positions' 61, 65, 67, 73, 74–75, 79
subjectivity 1–2, 9, 18, 26–27, 105; 'blank' 44, 45, 46, 47–48; 'complex' 44, 59–60, 61; Critical Discourse Analysis 19; dialectics 32; discourses 84; discursive complexes 60–62; ego-psychology 58; problems with discourse analysis 89; psychoanalysis 45, 49, 50–51, 52, 67, 73; readers 66; research process 3–4; researchers 45, 49, 55–56, 64; Semiotic Analysis 22; spiral of 35; 'uncomplicated' 44, 45, 46, 48–49; varieties of 59
subjects: agency 18; critical psychology 26; discourse analysis 46; discursive complexes 61; psychoanalysis 45, 49–50; texts 54
'Suprematism' 100
symbolic forms 99, 101

TA *see* Thematic Analysis
talk 10–11
texts 5, 16, 60, 90; bare 94–95; collective phenomena 53; discursive complexes 67–72, 73–75; as 'other' 45, 56–57; Political Discourse Theory 24, 25; problems of method 77, 78, 79; psychoanalysis 44–45, 52, 54–55, 61, 66–67; researcher subjectivity 55–56; Semiotic Analysis 22; variation, function and construction 64–66, 69
Thatcher, Margaret 25
Thematic Analysis (TA) 16–18, 23
theory 3, 4, 18; Conversation Analysis 11–12; empiricism 81; ethnomethodology 14; psychoanalysis 24; relativism 87
therapy 15, 28, 39, 40, 41
'three-sided football' 7
topic 29, 42
transcription 11, 12, 94–95, 101
trans-disciplinary research 9–10
transference 66, 67, 74
transformation 9, 10, 84
trauma 14–15, 18
trivialization 29–30, 42
truth: empiricism 81–82; postmodern turn 85; psychoanalytic theory 50; regimes of 45, 51, 57, 75

uncertainty 85
'uncomplicated subjectivity' 44, 45, 46, 48–49
the unconscious 23, 53–54, 58, 65
United States 32, 37, 58, 60, 104

variation 64, 65, 69
violence 69, 70, 71, 72
visual methodologies 22
Vološinov, V. 53
voluntarism 79, 84

war 92–93, 105
Western culture 26, 45, 50, 51–52, 58, 59–60, 61, 66, 67
Widdicombe, Sue 76
'wild analysis' 54
Wittgenstein, L. 46
The Wizard of Oz 35

Yugoslavia, former 97, 98, 100, 102, 104

Žižek, Slavoj 24, 50, 57, 58, 70, 74